ABSINTHE : A Journal of World Literature in Translation is published twice a year by the Department of Comparative Literature at the University of Michigan.

ABSINTHE : A Journal of World Literature in Translation receives the generous support of the following schools, offices and programs at the University of Michigan: Rackham Graduate School, Office of the Vice Provost for Global and Engaged Education, Institute for the Humanities, International Institute, Armenian Studies Program, and the Kenneth G. Lieberthal and Richard H. Rogel Center for Chinese Studies.

Correspondence should be addressed to

ABSINTHE : A Journal of World Literature in Translation
Department of Comparative Literature
2015 Tisch Hall
435 South State Street
Ann Arbor, MI 48109-1003

Typesetting and Design
William Kalvin, Delmas Typesetting. Ann Arbor, Michigan
delmastype.com

ISBN : 978-1-60785-480-7
ISSN : 1543-8449

sites.lsa.umich.edu/absinthe
Follow us on Twitter : @AbsintheJournal

ABSINTHE

WORLD LITERATURE IN TRANSLATION

UNSCRIPTED: AN ARMENIAN PALIMPSEST

ABSINTHE 23 | WINTER 2017

A selection by Tamar M. Boyadjian

ABSINTHE 23 TABLE OF CONTENTS

Tamar Boyadjian
1 From the Editor

Karén Karslyan
7 From *The Dark Side of the Week*

Tamar Boyadjian & Karén Karslyan
21 "Silent-Word City"

Krikor Beledian & Talar Chahinian
39 "In the Language of Catastrophe"

Vehanoush Tekian & Karen Jallatyan
51 "Forgive me for all those words"
53 "There will be silence in the museum and phantom of death"
55 "To explain without words"
57 "The ruins call intensely with their stubborn"

Christian Batikian & Tamar Boyadjian
61 "Winter Soldier"

Ara Kazandjian & Aram Kouyoumjian/Tamar Boyadjian
79 From *suspended line*

Ani Asatryan & Narine Jallatyan
87 "Words"

Shushan Avagyan & Milena Abrahamyan
101 "Blackselves"

Violet Grigoryan & Shushan Karapetian
125 "Buzz"

Eduard Hakhverdian & Lilit Keshishyan
147 "Prodigal Son"

Anna Davtyan
159 "In the name of Button"

Maroush Yeramian & Michael Pifer
165 "Aleppo, Aleppo"
170 "Without Exit"

Ikna Sariaslan & Alec Ekmekji
177 "West Side Story"
178 "Laborer of Love"
179 "LO"

Aram Pachyan & Nairi Hakhverdi
185 "Remembering the Reader"

Boghos Kupelian & Tamar Boyadjian/Roger Kupelian
195 "Black and White Moments"

Vahan Ishkhanyan & Dzovinar Derderian
207 From *Those Large, Blue Eyes*

Marc Nichanian
223 "Still Born: Repetition, Translation, and Translatability"

FROM THE EDITOR

When I was asked to compile a volume of Armenian literature in English translation, I was reminded of Antoine Berman and what he describes in his seminal work, *The Experience of the Foreign*, as the aim of translation: "Fertilizing what is one's own through the mediation of what is foreign." We can then consider translation as an aperture that allows us passage to the intricacies of a literary culture, to which the original language cannot grant us access. As Schlegel puts it, an aim that makes the "mother tongue" play.

One of the critical goals of this issue is to explore how translating allows for lacunas in texts to surface and function as possible palimpsests, opaquely inscribed over original works. And how these palimpsests survive as witnesses to a double cultural memory: a written testimony through which translating can make the same language and literature survive itself anew. This becomes an especially significant imperative for Western Armenian—a language of the diaspora, some even argue beyond a dialect (its own individual language) with no official nation, a tongue still spoken by those who survived one of the greatest genocides in human history.

How do we then translate literature built upon its own ruins? This volume is an inception into this question in its efforts to make Armenian translations (from its two main dialects: Western and Eastern Armenian) informants to the growing field of translation studies. This collection includes contemporary Armenian texts from living authors, chosen as significant works that challenge, shape, and complicate conversations on transcultural analysis, and theories and practices related to translating. For this reason, you will find at the end of each translation an afterthought by the translator on the process of translating that particular work within the context of larger questions surrounding translation and translatability.

The lack of compelling translations from the Armenian language into English has oftentimes deterred scholars working across multiple fields from considering Armenian literature alongside the literatures of other cultures.

This issue invites translators to move beyond purely prescriptive applications of translation, interpretation, and the localization of national literatures—and the mere translation of a "minor" literature into a major language—to consider their translations of contemporary Armenian literature as part of larger, non-compartmentalized cultural and theoretical frameworks and disciplines such as comparative literature, Mediterranean studies, Postcolonial studies, Diaspora studies, Trauma studies, and others. Translators have also reflected upon questions pertaining to the ethics of semiotic and cultural translation, and what ways (if possible) cultural nuances transform and translate across linguistic, political, and literary mediums. Several authors in the volume have also engaged in self-translation, exploring how an author's own engagement with their text in a different language exposes an intimacy veiled in the characters of the original.

While they by no means comprise an exhaustive list, the following pages provide a survey of contemporary and active writers from around the world in Armenian at present day. Here, we have a corpus of writers mostly from the Armenian Diaspora–Lebanon, Syria, Iran, the United States, France, Sierra Leone—and some from the Republic of Armenia. Their translations grant access to an Armenian literary present and past, while at the same time allowing others to enter this same world. This volume imagines texts and translations as being weighed against one another as balancing acts of statements and silences. Whereas translations have traditionally been viewed as granting access to others, here we also see the alluring possibility of unmasking the unspoken in Armenian literature, to reveal mutual secrets unraveled in the movements between one language and another. *Unscripted: An Armenian Palimpsest* is an attempt to break the secrecy of our own language by translating the unspoken, to pulsate the silence beyond letters and words to a readership that is yet to receive it—the world of the original and its recreation; a world where our (same) language lives as a surviving one.

I thank the *Absinthe* team as well as the Armenian Studies Program at the University of Michigan for helping this incredibly significant volume come to fruition. And a special thanks to all the contributing authors and translators without whom this volume would not be possible.

DR. TAMAR M. BOYADJIAN
MICHIGAN STATE UNIVERSITY

KARÉN KARSLYAN

From *The Dark Side of the Week*

(poetry)

Translated by the Author

The Dark Side of the Week[1]

Monnight
Tuesnight
Wednesnight
Thursnight
Frinight
Saturnight
Sunnight

da

y

d
a

[1]This entire collection consists of a couple dozen pairs of poems, where every second poem is the dream of the preceding one. Thus, "The Fragrance of Lampposts" is the dream of "The Dark Side of the Week," and "A Picture Is Worth a Thousand Words" is the dream of "Black Paper."

The Fragrance of Lampposts

Too many brooms in this room
No room to sweep the floor
Tzling
        Tzling
                Tzling
Complained the overhanging hollow copper pipes
A head had brushed against them
A right eye scraped
A security video camera lens
Colors trespassed the outlines
The bristles of the brooms blossomed

A dog was lying on its back in front of my door
A lady disappeared behind a lamppost
The dog was struggling like a ladybug
To get back on its numerous
Wriggling chaotic legs
The lady walked on with that lamppost
In her hand and picked a few
More as she walked by

I landed the tip of my little finger on the ground
The dog climbed it up
But slipped and fell on its back again
Its paws were feebly rotating in the air
Like the blades of a broken propeller

The woman buried her nose
Into the bunch of lampposts
And smelled the blinding lights
She looked happy
Faceless

The street plunged into darkness
I lay on my back next to the struggling dog
A flock of woodpeckers flew over us
Into the room of the blooming brooms

Black Paper[2]

Poetry is dead
I killed it
Read the email
I received from a group of
Familiar American poets
I love it when they poke post-post-modern fun
At grandiose notions of the past

Zeus cleaved them into inferior males and females
When the superior androgynes tried to kill Him
After Nietzsche pronounced God dead
The latter drove him insane
Without producing any proof of
The fact of His own existence

Poets killing poetry
Subconscious claim to be Überpoets?

We are nihilistic thoughts
Occurring in non-existent God's brain

Supersonic fighters
Shoot themselves down
By accelerating to top speed
And into the asses of their own fired missiles
War shatters to pieces

[2]During WWII, a Soviet official letter announcing a soldier's death had black margins. In Armenia, such letters were dubbed as "black paper."

Peace is a collage made of those smithereens
My love has the shape not of heart
But fractured lines

Poetry is dead
They say

If poetry is dead
I am a necrophile

A Picture is Worth a Thousand Words

This poem is now worth zero point five percent of a picture
This poem is now worth one point seven percent of a picture
This poem is now worth two point nine percent of a picture
This poem is now worth four point one percent of a picture
This poem is now worth five point three percent of a picture
This poem is now worth six point five percent of a picture
This poem is now worth seven point seven percent of a picture
This poem is now worth eight point nine percent of a picture
This poem is now worth ten point one percent of a picture
This poem is now worth eleven point three percent of a picture
This poem is now worth twelve point five percent of a picture
This poem is now worth thirteen point seven percent of a picture
This poem is now worth fourteen point nine percent of a picture
This poem is now worth sixteen point one percent of a picture
This poem is now worth seventeen point three percent of a picture
This poem is now worth eighteen point five percent of a picture
This poem is now worth nineteen point seven percent of a picture
This poem is now worth twenty point nine percent of a picture

This poem is now worth twenty-two point one percent of a
picture
This poem is now worth twenty-three point four percent of a
picture
This poem is now worth twenty-four point seven percent of a
picture
This poem is now worth twenty-six percent of a picture
This poem is now worth twenty-seven point one percent of a
picture
This poem is now worth twenty-eight point four percent of a
picture
This poem is now worth twenty-nine point seven percent of a
picture
This poem is now worth thirty-one percent of a picture
This poem is now worth thirty-two point one percent of a
picture
This poem is now worth thirty-three point four percent of a
picture
This poem is now worth thirty-four point seven percent of a
picture
This poem is now worth thirty-six percent of a picture
This poem is now worth thirty-seven point one percent of a
picture
This poem is now worth thirty-eight point four percent of a
picture
This poem is now worth thirty-nine point seven percent of a
picture
This poem is now worth fourty-one percent of a picture
This poem is now worth fourty-two point one percent of a
picture

This poem is now worth fourty-three point four percent of a picture
This poem is now worth fourty-four point seven percent of a picture
This poem is now worth fourty-six percent of a picture
This poem is now worth fourty-seven point one percent of a picture
This poem is now worth forty-eight point four percent of a picture
This poem is now worth forty-nine point seven percent of a picture
This poem is now worth fifty-one percent of a picture
This poem is now worth fifty-two point one percent of a picture
This poem is now worth fifty-three point four percent of a picture
This poem is now worth fifty-four point seven percent of a picture
This poem is now worth fifty-six percent of a picture
This poem is now worth fifty-seven point one percent of a picture
This poem is now worth fifty-eight point four percent of a picture
This poem is now worth fifty-nine point seven percent of a picture
This poem is now worth sixty-one percent of a picture
This poem is now worth sixty-two point one percent of a picture
This poem is now worth sixty-three point four percent of a picture

This poem is now worth sixty-four point seven percent of a
picture
This poem is now worth sixty-six percent of a picture
This poem is now worth sixty-seven point one percent of a
picture
This poem is now worth sixty-eight point four percent of a
picture
This poem is now worth sixty-nine point seven percent of a
picture
This poem is now worth seventy-one percent of a picture
This poem is now worth seventy-two point one percent of a
picture
This poem is now worth seventy-three point four percent of a
picture
This poem is now worth seventy-four point seven percent of a
picture
This poem is now worth seventy-six percent of a picture
This poem is now worth seventy-seven point one percent of a
picture
This poem is now worth seventy-eight point four percent of a
picture
This poem is now worth seventy-nine point seven percent of
a picture
This poem is now worth eighty-one percent of a picture
This poem is now worth eighty-two point one percent of a
picture
This poem is now worth eighty-three point four percent of a
picture
This poem is now worth eighty-four point seven percent of a
picture

This poem is now worth eighty-six percent of a picture
This poem is now worth eighty-seven point one percent of a picture
This poem is now worth eighty-eight point four percent of a picture
This poem is now worth eighty-nine point seven percent of a picture
This poem is now worth ninety-one percent of a picture
This poem is now worth ninety-two point one percent of a picture
This poem is now worth ninety-three point four percent of a picture
This poem is now worth ninety-four point seven percent of a picture
This poem is now worth ninety-six percent of a picture
This poem is now worth ninety-seven point one percent of a picture
This poem is now worth ninety-eight point four percent of a picture
This poem is now worth ninety-nine point seven percent of a picture
This poem is now worth more than a picture

I write in Armenian and in English. I translate my own works into these languages and Russian. I start translating my writings while they are still in progress, because translation is an important tool for my creative process. I draw inspiration and ideas from the peculiarities of grammatical logic, the etymological pool, and the phonetic power of each of these languages as I write the next stanza, next line, or next word. Thus, translating various parts of a poem at various stages of the writing process invariably alters its course. Though language can be perceived as clothing for a poem, I tailor not only a language to a poem, but also vice versa.

Upon completion of a poem, I make sure it is represented in each language as accurately as a literary translation may possibly be, just shy of Nabokov's extreme approach "the clumsiest of literal translation is a thousand times more useful than prettiest of paraphrase"—and, at the same time, steering clear of the other extreme method mentioned by Edward FitzGerald—"the live Dog better than the dead Lion."[3]

Karén Karslyan

[3]As quoted by Sachin Ketkar in "Literary Translation: Recent Theoretical Developments."

TAMAR BOYADJIAN

"Silent Word-City"

(poetry)

With an accompanying essay by Karén Karslyan

un

"He is not only an interpreter of the play of dissimulation who can be likened to one who exposes letters; he or it is also in the place of what is called here being or the letter [*l'être ou lettre*] . . ."
(Jacques Derrida, from *The Gift of Death*)

We are constantly asked to think about the way in which technology can build a future, but we have forgotten that once writing was considered to be technological, and more importantly that systems of writing are forms of visual art. But today I take for granted the graphic expansion of the word; or that the word, the letter, is in and of itself a symbol of power. And I substitute the essence behind word, letter, phrase—a meaning imposed on me through language itself (a hegemonic language), that relies on that same system that once was considered artistic and revolutionary.

You know what I am trying to reify through these (blank) verbal constructs? Here I wander through to the language of the city. The spoken and (un-)spoken. The technological and graphic. The grid of the building blocks that simultaneously form and (de-)form. For is not naming un-naming? Does it not depend on whose name we (you) are using? Does it not rely on the language *you* are naming *me* with? I am forced to speak through you: Your language; do you even hear me? Since when I speak (on) my own you, pretend you don't understand me? Sometimes (because of you), I can't even understand myself anymore.

What is the language of my city? Whose light shines through
  my calligraphic infrastructures

isolating

me

The incest of imposition has made me mute:
I can only methodologically copy (your) script now

Seems; It will always remain in your hand

I try to relieve it by cutting it off . . .
it may rehabilitate itself anew through the curvatures
drawn with my conduit pen.

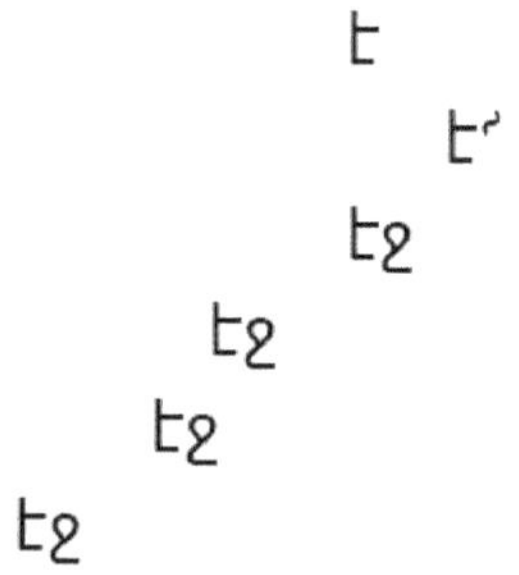

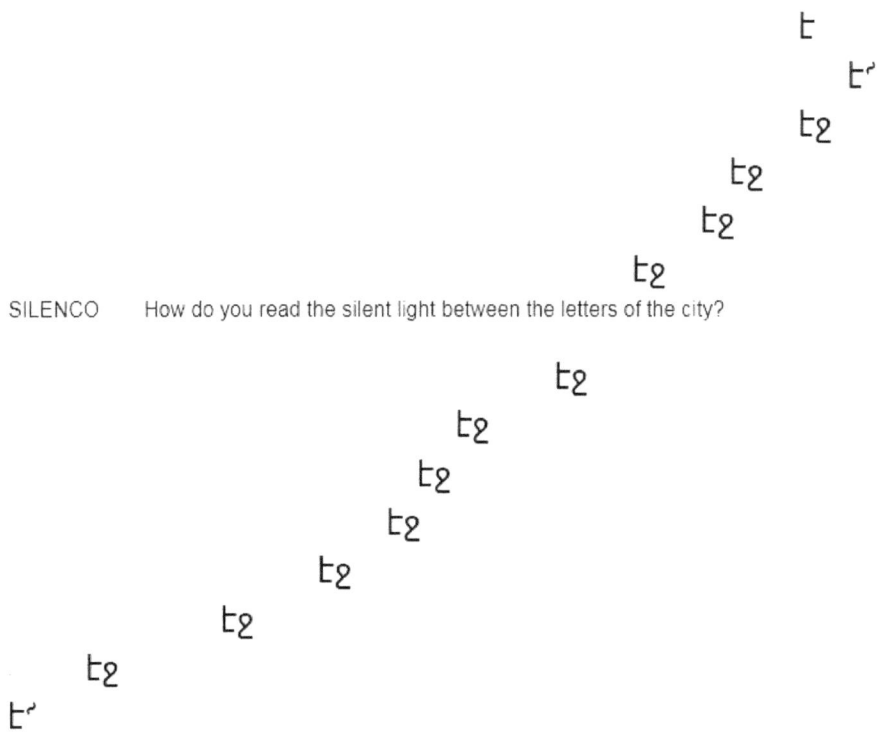

SILENCO How do you read the silent light between the letters of the city?

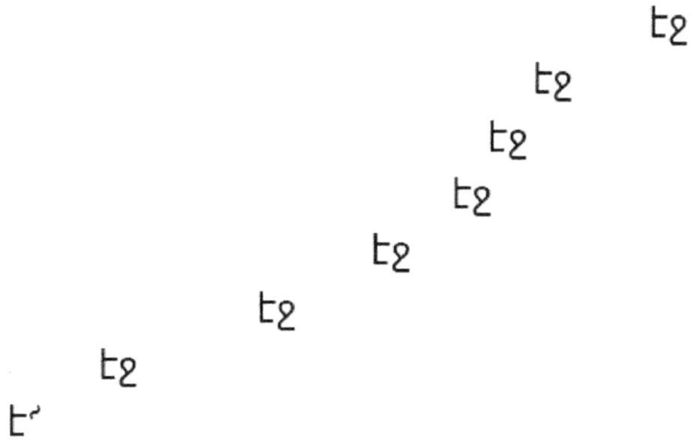

ɭnju ; unɭu

La lumière ; de Monde

Ⴈnɭn النور ; نور ElĿnor

hell;; licht ; leicht Erhellen

φως ;

Φotoς ελαφρύ

lumen ; limen

luce ; ɭnɭծĿ

lapsus

u

VALO

VALO

Վայլէ́

I do not speak as I have spoken:
that
paralyzing uncontended truth
a prosthetic linguistics
perspect vises

in:
to

submissive
oblivion

I do not hear as I have been heard:
that
city of (un-)masquerading truth
unveiled
a silent madness
prevails wise

in
to:

(in-)controlled
absent

crescent   wounds.

Was the fate of the lost letter?

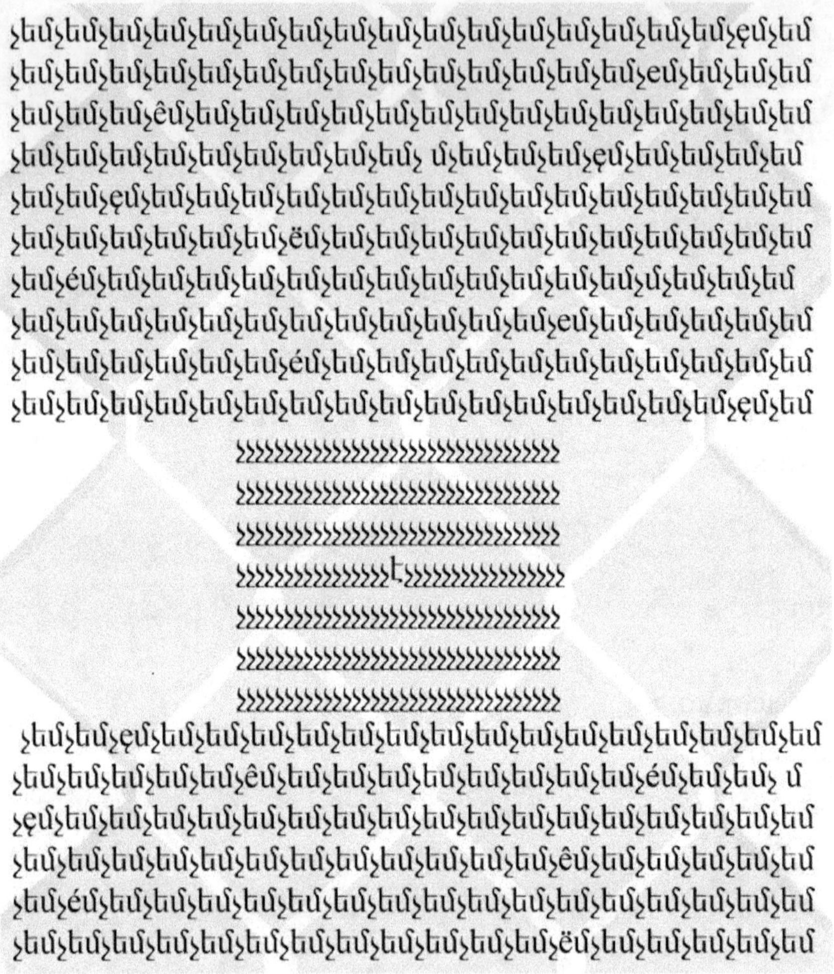

Intertextual Crossroads in Tamar Boyadjian's "Silent Word-City"

What does the enormous Armenian lowercase letter "տ" at the very beginning of the poem stand for? By first warning readers that we have forgotten that "systems of writing are forms of visual art, the poem hacks our default perception of graphemes. This reminder takes us back to the very beginning of the poem and shines a light on the visual attributes of the enormous Armenian small letter "տ." As a visual element, it looks like two halves of an oval symbol placed next to each other. And when placed one upon the other, the two halves resemble the Latin "D," which is, in fact, the phonetic equivalent of the Western Armenian letter "տ." The epigraph seems to hold a key as to what it may stand for, at least, as a grapheme. Moreover, the manner in which it is presented in the epigraph is itself another key:

> *He is not only an interpreter of the play of dissimulation who can be likened to one who exposes letters: he or it is also in the place of what is called here being or the letter [l'être ou lettre].*[1]

Who is "he"? The latter is identified in the sentence preceding the quoted one, but which is left out by Boyadjian:

> *Heidegger himself, and his work, come to resemble a purloined letter. He is not only an interpreter of the play of dissimulation who can be likened to one who exposes letters; he or it is also in the place of what is called here being or the letter [l'être ou lettre].*[2]

In this quote from Gift of Death, *Derrida refers to Patočka's reluctance to straightforwardly quote Heidegger in his essay*

---

[1]Derrida, Jacques. *The Gift of Death*. Trans. David Wills. Chicago: U of Chicago Press, 1995, p. 39.
[2]*Ibid.*

"Is Technological Civilization Decadent, and Why?" According to Derrida, the Czech philosopher alludes to Heidegger in "a strangely encrypted form."[3] *He likens Patočka's strategy of reference to that employed by Minister D– in Poe's* Purloined Letter, *that is, leaving something in plain sight as an effective method of concealment. So, does "*un*" stand for Minister D– or does it imply Mr. Dupin, the detective who was able to find and recover the purloined letter?*

The "purloined letter" was originally evoked by Patočka, in the same essay, to describe how "force manifests itself as the highest concealment of Being."[4] *Like Mr. Dupin, Derrida picks up the reference left in plain sight and turns it toward Patočka himself, who thereby is transformed into that very force that conceals the Being, which, here, is Heidegger.*

*Boyadjian, in carefully chiseling her epigraph, as if reconstructing Patočka's play of dissimulation, reinstates the Mystery by re-hiding Heidegger, albeit in plain sight. Such an act echoes Patočka's statement: "The most sophisticated inventions are boring if they do not lead to an exacerbation of the Mystery (*Tajemstvi*) concealed by what we discover, what is revealed to us)."*[5] *Or does Boyadjian, by re-enacting exposed concealment, thus associate herself with Minister D– (Minister D ou Minister* un*), a poet about whose clever trick philosophers have been since raving. Is Boyadjian's self-identification with Minister D– inspired by his ingenious demonstration that underestimation of poets inevitably leads to failure? This was insinuated by Dupin*

[3] Derrida, Jacques. *The Gift of Death & Literature in secret*. Trans. David Wills. 2nd ed. Chicago, IL: U of Chicago Press, 2008, p. 39.
[4] *Ibid.*
[5] *Ibid.*, p. 37.

who ascribed the policemen's inability to find the letter to such underestimation: "As poet and mathematician, he would reason well; as mere mathematician, he could not have reasoned at all, and thus would have been at the mercy of the Prefect."[6] Doesn"t Boyadjian therefore become the "force" that conceals the Being, Minister D–? The enormous "ա" seems to stand also for the Being (although the first letter is different).

At any rate, "ա" is but a letter Boyadjian has purloined from the Armenian alphabet. But what else might this enormous purloined letter encompass besides Derrida, Minister D–, Mr. Dupin, the Being? If Heidegger is, for Derrida, not only an interpreter, the detective who exposed the purloined letters—perhaps also himself the purloined letter—then one of Boyadjian's most visually conspicuous elements, the enormous "ա," is the "trumpery filigree card-rack of pasteboard, that hung dangling by a dirty blue ribbon, from a little brass knob just beneath the middle of the mantelpiece"—Minister D–'s hiding place of choice for the purloined letter.

But the speaker of "Silent Word-City" is in a quest for another purloined entity. It could be described as a purloined l'être. As prompted by the title, it is the silent word loosely defined by Stéphane Mallarmé as follows (in Boyadjian's translation):

> *[. . .] the immortal word remains silent; the diversity of idioms on earth prevents everybody from uttering the words which, otherwise, at one single stroke, would materialize as truth.*[7]

---

[6]Poe, Edgar Alan. "The Purloined Letter by Edgar Allan Poe." *American Studies at the University of Virginia.* Web. 15 Feb. 2017. <http://xroads.virginia.edu/~hyper/poe/purloine.html>.

[7]Boyadjian, Tamar M. *"Is Not Translation, but a quest for some . . ." Makukachu: Anthology of Contemporary Armenian Literature.* Grigoryan, Violet, and Vahan Ishkhanyan, comps. Ed. Tamar M. Boyadjian. Yerevan, Ingnagir Literary Club, 2016, p. 8.

In other words, all the languages have purloined the immortal silent word by the sheer fact of their existence. And the diversity of idioms, the existence of world languages, is but a play of dissimulation to hide the silent word. In this context, Boyadjian's engagement of multiple languages or diverse idioms in her texts, including "Silent Word-City," is perhaps an unconscious subliminal message that the silent word, the ultimate truth, is always lurking in the open, in all of her texts. Much like Minister D–'s purloined letter, the immortal silent word will speak the truth if uttered, publicized. Boyadjian strives to utter it by exercising what Patočka calls "an exacerbation of the Mystery."

The Armenian language is one of the roughly 6,500 accomplices in the conspiracy to purloin the immortal silent word. Boyadjian summons the Armenian, her native tongue, in her quest of the purloined l'être (ou lettre). Into her otherwise English text she imports the Armenian capital "Է," the seventh lettre of the alphabet, which not only sounds like "ê" in l'être, but also means the latter: "Being," "Creature," "Essence." Furthermore, in Armenian religious vocabulary, "Է" means "God."

The placement of "Է" in the poem is noteworthy. It appears above the following sentence: "How do you read the silent light between the letters of the city?" Morphing into the word "Էջ" —meaning both "page" and "downward motion"— the letter/word "Է" flows "between the letters" of the question and continues its fall through the poem between more and more letters. As the fall continues, it more and more resembles that of Alice through the rabbit hole, by virtue of its slow, explorative nature.

While Alice was falling past the bookshelves, "Է" is effectively *falling through texts, between their letters. The first phase of the fall is through a circular "calligraphic infrastructure" filled with blinding light. This segment of the poem is likely an answer to a question set earlier: "What is the language of my city? Whose light shines through my calligraphic infrastructures." Though the speaker reckons with the powers of the ubiquitous language, she struggles to identify it. Not only does she not know whose light shines, but also how to read that silent light between the letters of the city.*

*Boyadjian links Mallarmé's concept of "silent word" to "light" as a symbol of "enlightenment," "knowledge." Thus, the round-shaped text starts with the Armenian words for "light" and "hush." Graphically, these words also contain letters that resemble the Armenian letter "*ա*" split in two— "*լոյս*" [luys] and "*սուս*" [soos]. The second phrase, "La lumière ; de Monde," is reminiscent of how Jesus referred to his disciples when addressing them – "La lumière du Monde" (Matthew 5:14).*

*The Armenian word for "pomegranate" (*նուռ*), in the following line, seems to go astray from the topic of light and silence, however, it bridges "*سبک*," the Farsi and Arabic word for "light," which sounds like the Armenian word for pomegranate (*նուռ* – noor). "*سبک*" is followed by "*النور*," which is Eleanora spelled in Farsi. This is where we encounter the second concrete reference to Poe, specifically, to his short story of the same name.*

Poe uses many metaphors of light (e.g. a Seraphim who has "an inextinguishable light,"[8] according to Thomas Aquinas) to

[8]Aquinas, Thomas. "Summa Theologica." *Documenta Catholica Omnia.* Web. 8 Feb. 2017. <http://www.documentacatholicaomnia.eu/03d/1225-1274,_Thomas_Aquinas,_Summa_Theologiae_%5B1%5D,_EN.pdf>.

describe Eleonora, which means "light of God" in Arabic. Apparently, Boyadjian chose Farsi to spell Eleonora, because the latter borrowed the style of "the songs of Schiraz"[9] to dwell upon a "sorrowful theme."[10] Interestingly, the Armenian "Է" replaces the letter "e" in between the letters of "El" and "nor," as if to place Being or Essence between God and Light.

The next line in "Silent Word-City" starts with what, at first, seems to be an antonym of light—"hell," whereas it is, in fact, the German word for "luminous." But this little linguistic confusion packs the drama and, perhaps, the culmination of the whole narrative. It is the metaphor for the burning and tormenting thoughts of this protagonist before eventually marrying Ermengarde against the vows he had given Eleonora before her death. One night, however, Eleonora's voice absolves him of his vows, evoking the reign and rule of the "Spirit of Love" a result of his action. Boyadjian has zipped this transformation, or the unexpected change of course, into a single word: "hell." Her choice to switch to German may be in honor of Ermengarde—a name of German origin, which means "universal protection."

On the one hand, the last German word in that line, "Erhellen"—"to light up," "to illuminate"—shares remote phonetic similarities with Ermengarde; on the other hand, Ermengarde may be interpreted as "Armenian protection" or "Protected Armenian" as "Ermeni" is Turkish for "Armenian." Does Ermengarde, in this sense, refer to the Armenian "Է" which appears well-guarded inside "ElԷnor," between God and Light?

9Poe, Edgar Alan. "Eleonora." *Lit2Go*. Web. 8 Feb. 2017. <http://etc.usf.edu/lit2go/147/the-works-of-edgar-allan-poe/5236/eleonora/>
10*Ibid.*

This accentuated relatedness of these two beings via their names offers a hint at what Eleonora is going to tell the protagonist in Heaven—that Eleonora and Ermengarde are identical or, paraphrasing Patočka, Ermengarde manifests herself as the highest concealment of Eleonora.

*Interestingly, the English reading of the German word "hell" (adj. light) corrupts the further reading experience. So, instead of interpreting the Armenian word "*լուծէ*" [loo-dzeh] as an order to solve, one is tempted to read it as an order to "carry out abnormal frequent intestinal evacuations with fluid stools." "*Լուծէ*" is preceded by "luce," the similarly sounding Italian word for light. Boyadjian also shines light to the homograph of "light" (not heavy) by inserting "leicht" (German) and "ελαφρύ" (Greek). Interestingly, the latter bears slight phonetic semblance of Eleonora. Near the end of this round-shaped section, Boyadjian introduces the Finnish word for light, "valo," which is followed by the similarly sounding (albeit slightly corrupted spelling) Armenian word "*Վայլէ*" [vahy-leh], which means "Enjoy!"*

*While Boyadjian tries hard to read "the silent light between the letters of the city" with the arsenal of "diverse idioms," "*է*" continues its fall through the words: "El*է*nor," "*լուծէ*," and "*Վայլէ*." Eventually, "*է*" finds itself, at the very bottom, surrounded by a plethora of the letter "*չ*" [ch]—the 25th letter of the Armenian alphabet, which signifies negation, the Armenian equivalent of "not," "un-," or "non-."*

չեմչեմչեմչեմչեմչեմչեմչեմչեմչեմչեմչեմչեմչեմչեմչեմչեմչեմչçմչեմ
չեմչեմչեմչեմչեմչեմչեմչեմչեմչեմչեմչեմչեմչեմչեմչեմչeմչեմչեմչեմ
չեմչեմչեմչêմչեմչեմչեմչեմչեմչեմչեմչեմչեմչեմչեմչեմչեմչեմչեմչեմ
չեմչեմչեմչեմչեմչեմչեմչեմչեմչեմչ մչեմչեմչçմչեմչեմչեմչեմչեմ
չեմչեմչçմչեմչեմչեմչեմչեմչեմչեմչեմչեմչեմչեմչեմչեմչեմչեմչեմչեմ
չեմչեմչեմչեմչեմչëմչեմչեմչեմչեմչեմչեմչեմչեմչեմչեմչեմչեմչեմչեմ
չեմչéմչեմչեմչեմչեմչեմչեմչեմչեմչեմչեմչեմչեմչեմչմչեմչեմչեմ
չեմչեմչեմչեմչեմչեմչեմչեմչեմչեմչեմչեմչեմչեմչեմչeմչեմչեմչեմչեմ
չեմչեմչեմչեմչեմչեմչեմչéմչեմչեմչեմչեմչեմչեմչեմչեմչեմչեմչեմչեմ
չեմչեմչեմչեմչեմչեմչեմչեմչեմչեմչեմչեմչեմչեմչեմչեմչեմչեմչçմչեմ

չչչչչչչչչչչչչչչչչչչչչչչչչչչչչչչչչ
չչչչչչչչչչչչչչչչչչչչչչչչչչչչչչչչ
չչչչչչչչչչչչչչչչչչչչչչչչչչչչչչչչ
չչչչչչչչչչչչչչչչէչչչչչչչչչչչչչչչչ
չչչչչչչչչչչչչչչչչչչչչչչչչչչչչչչչ
չչչչչչչչչչչչչչչչչչչչչչչչչչչչչչչչ
չչչչչչչչչչչչչչչչչչչչչչչչչչչչչչչչ

չեմչեմչçմչեմչեմչեմչեմչեմչեմչեմչեմչեմչեմչեմչեմչեմչեմչեմչեմչեմ
չեմչեմչեմչեմչեմչêմչեմչեմչեմչեմչեմչեմչեմչեմչéմչեմչեմչ մ
չçմչեմչեմչեմչեմչեմչեմչեմչեմչեմչեմչեմչեմչեմչեմչեմչեմչեմչեմչեմ
չեմչեմչեմչեմչեմչեմչեմչեմչեմչեմչեմչեմչեմչեմչեմչեմչêմչեմչեմչեմ
չեմչéմչեմչեմչեմչեմչեմչեմչեմչեմչեմչեմչեմչեմչեմչեմչեմչեմչեմչեմ
չեմչեմչեմչեմչեմչեմչեմչեմչեմչեմչեմչեմչեմչեմչեմչեմչëմչեմչեմչեմ

That small square of negations surrounding the symbol of Being, Essence or God, is itself situated between two larger rectangles at the top and at the bottom. Both rectangles contain the repetition of the Armenian word for "am not," where the 5th Armenian letter "Ե" (which, here, is pronounced "Է") is occasionally replaced by the familiar "ê" from "l'être." And this entire structure is in the shape of the English "I," which, thus, reads "I am not."

*Here, at the end of "Silent Word-City," it is as hard to forget that "systems of writing are forms of visual art," as it is to "take for granted the graphic expansion of the word." This monumental "calligraphic infrastructure" is the total negation of the Self—its total destruction in the hopes of attaining the silent word. It is the destruction of "l'être" by "lettres." This vaguely echoes the following statement at the beginning of "Silent Word-City": "And I substitute the essence behind word, letter, phrase -a meaning imposed on me through language." The apparent reversal of this statement at the end—the graphic self-negation or "(in)controlled / absent," where "the essence behind word, letter, phrase" negate the "I" that was supposed to substitute them—throws the poem into an endless loop of a Möbius strip. The loop is also reinforced thanks to the fact that the giant Armenian letter "*տ*" at the very beginning of "Silent Word-City" is a negative prefix just like the Armenian letter "*չ*" at the very end.*

Karén Karslyan

KRIKOR BELEDIAN

"In the Language of Catastrophe"

(non-fiction)

Translated by Talar Chahinian

How prosaic an event, that is to say, the annihilation of a community, of a people. How domestic, how familial an affair. Some have reached me only by name, I know little or nothing about these people and remain suspended from these unknown faces of mine. Since childhood, I have heard about their disappearance, at times gruesome stories transmitted from familiar and unfamiliar mouths, repeated and scattered, fairy tales parents tell to put their children to sleep. Collective extermination has its private side. From the outset, I burn in its narrative. It is for this reason that I often prefer to remain silent. Not because there is nothing to say or that I shudder before what happened, in its magnitude or its impossibility, which are both partly true; but rather because how can you speak of your planned and consummated annihilation? What circumstances have contrived as such that your father, at age seven, is orphaned, but saved; your mother, at age three, is orphaned and saved, then they meet and bear you? Your story begins in such circumstances. Through which your origin becomes a catastrophe and an escape from it. That we lived is a miracle, they would say. Not that god intervened, for there was no god, neither before it, neither during those scorching years, nor afterward; instead the orphans simply endured the crime, the starvation, the heat and the cold, the beatings, the malaria, the famine, and the madness. Those who pass through fire become like hammered metal, a survivor once said. But it comes at a price. They lost everything; they had no identity, they forgot their language, but they did not forget that they came from a certain place, that they were exiled, and that there, where we used to live, here dispersed, was not our place. What were our predecessors to give us if not that which they themselves did not have or the only thing they did have, the traces of catastrophe. Themselves.

Themselves: inheritance and legacy.

The scholar escapes from it. He refuses to inherit the impossibility to live, that free, arguable, irresponsible, idle existence. He refuses mourning and lament. He is accustomed to that through the centuries. Same old story. The storyteller said long ago, *they distanced us from our occupation*. And they would not accept seeing so much as our shadows. We . . . shadowy beings or non-beings. But the scholar writes. Writing is a connection to life, a form of communication that eludes the dead. Then again, what is language? Communication. Only in poetry is it otherwise. It is only itself, that is to say uniform, unprotected, powerful and weak at the same time. What is the use of poetry if placed against and within this nullity?

As is often the case, that which you would forget, that which you would escape, follows you. It confronts you in the most unexpected place. As though it would not have you abandon it and speak. For the scholar, language is that place where he works, upon which he toils, and through which he becomes himself. There, he feels safe. Or he thinks himself protected. You can spread doubt about the capabilities of language, but then you think, language belongs to you. And therein occurs the event, simultaneously old and new, the imperishable. That which you sought to forget appears—nightmare, dream, delirium. The catastrophe is in the language. I do not wish to say that the genocide is a linguistic phenomenon, that it does not exist, that it is not an historical event. A metaphysical fiction. Until now, I have spoken of physics, or one might say of testimony. Only from experience. I said the catastrophe is in the language, it is there. The scholar did not know it. He learned it.

The gruesome stories have come from the mouths of survivors; they came to me when I knew nothing of the world. During long winter nights, the elders would gather around the fire, while the children slept a bit farther away in the same room. Some of the elders would begin to tell their stories, while others would form an audience. The children would either sleep or feign sleep. In anticipation of horror and wonderous warmth. We knew everything and we had to repeat everything again. The mark of memory remains ineffaceable like a brand. And one day, when the storytellers spoke at length and a hush fell over the audience, when a certain general meditation was established, at that very moment, around the faint fire, the Erzrumtsi, who played the gray-haired grandmother to us, interrupted the speech:

> What you chitter-chattering on about? Them there took away our tongue, what more could'a we give up?

It is always hard to believe that we spoke, more or less, that language. That presumably unbroken language. Our ears were filled with the dialects of the provinces. And at school they taught us the clean, beautiful literary Armenian. Because we had to grow up and be men. As if unshattered, unbroken. We had to arrive at language, as though one way or another we were going to deny what happened. No, we had not died, we had not been resurrected. No matter what, we existed, and not only that, but we multiplied. Ankara radio had been locked and sealed shut. But the listener would always hear that ineffaceable, deafening sound of the victor.

The writer wants to become a scholar.

Of course he studies his language, as though it were completely alive. He also learns a few dialects. He can name the world. He realizes, he realizes slowly with disdain that he speaks, hears, and writes a language that has passed through fire, that has been saved from the desert's burn, but that is a remnant, a residue, a part of a corpse. Beautiful, sublime, amazing, but . . . a scrap from a rag, a bead, a hairpin, like those one might find in the sand, after a storm. An archeological find.

I know, the talkers will object; while chewing gum, they will announce that it is not right. What of the glorious language as a native land, language as home? I said early on that I will speak of an intimate matter, a matter for scholars. This is not a national issue, nor is it a familial affair. It is my experience with language or my burn from our language. Mine is a language that has eluded catastrophe and not a language of those who survived from it. A shadowy thing, like when the truth explodes. The catastrophe, which I used to think of as an event, as a distant story, has reached our mouths; it has cut our tongue. They pulled out our tongue, said the last *khanum* of the Erzrum clan. It turns out she was more knowledgeable, wiser than I thought. More sound than the archive and the witness, seeking truth and rejoicing in disaster. Evidence for the catastrophe as a linguistic phenomenon abounds, beginning with the fetishization of language, the demand or command to speak in a purified tongue, the sanctification of the alphabet, the acclaim, all of which we needed in order to preserve a portion of the language. Is language not a relic? To either place in your mouth or put in a cabinet like consecrated, sacramental bread. You dare not throw it away.

The German poet has said,

> We are a sign, without meaning,
>
> And we nearly lost our language in alienation.

It is understandable that we lose the language when its place disappears, when its country essentially vanishes from sight, unguarded and forbidden. Language becomes abandoned, a dialect stripped of land, something I have called "unpeopled language." Almost, meaning not entirely, which at the same time is already the whole.

When I said language, I did not have only a means of communication in mind, rather a means of reflection as well. An intellectual price was assigned to the catastrophe, said a surviving writer. I am not thinking only about the intellectuals who were killed or vanished in 1915. I am also thinking about the ability to form thoughts, to ponder, to visualize the occurrence, to bring it to meaning or to significance. Reflection was deferred. The victims had no need for it, they needed to survive. With an invalid and elemental fervor. Now, years later, in a time when all sorts of denial and refutation are freely at work, we remember our own extermination sometimes in horror, sometimes in awe, and sometimes in envy. We realize that we are not yet able to speak it. While understanding it, we have not yet been able to comprehend it. We have not yet reached its level or its abyss or its base. It has not had time to ripen.

The scholar hears only the shadowy language, what can he do? Destroy his pen and remain silent? Move to another language, to give testimony in that language? A second language? Is it not key to establish to the world that once we were not and now we are? This is a question of choice. A scholar can write in whichever language he chooses, as long as he truly has options. I choose to write in the language that genocidal will sought to erase. In other words, the language of the victim. Neither elegant nor majestic. This is not an attempt to attest to the past existence of the language. In that case, writing would become a folkloric act. A retrograde carnival. The scholar does not choose such solutions. They are simple. To revive? He is not Christ to resurrect Lazarus. Christ, too, is devoid of the body necessary for miracles. Christ is empty. Writing is not an informal form of worship, and certainly not a consecration. All the words are there, indiscriminately. Crime, genocide, catastrophe, disaster, and others. But the scholar knows that the names mask the only unnamed, the only name not found in words. The missing. The internal shape of the mind. The scholar does not refute, he does not judge or condemn, nor does he forgive. He does not concern himself with amends and consolation, souls at peace or with wounds. He searches for the supreme sentence.

When the critic imagines, he remembers. When he remembers, he presides, without chrism or mass, over not so much tradition, cultural riches and other crucial areas, as language. The dead body needs someone to watch over it, they say; a killer in other words, so that it can disconnect entirely and become itself. There are those who fall silent, while others lament. Between these two creeps the desire to write, crude and unrelenting, and it mourns. The desire is infinite, like the catastrophe, it has no end. But writing is not a writable catastrophe.

Krikor Beledian published "In the Language of Catastrophe" on the occasion of the Armenian genocide's centennial in April 2015. The short think-piece reflects on the impact of catastrophe on language. More specifically, it focuses on the impossible task of reinstituting the Western Armenian linguistic form in exile. His rendering of catastrophe as the death of language, or of dialects, represents the culmination of the author's decades-long meditation on catastrophe, developed through his multiple volumes of poetry, prose, and criticism.

Born and raised in Lebanon, Krikor Beledian moved to Paris in the late 1960s in pursuit of higher education and stayed there to develop his literary career. Though detached from the Armenian enclave of Beirut that has sustained an exclusively Armenian-speaking population, Beledian has become a leading figure in contemporary Armenian literature. Aside from his critical writings, some of which are published in French, Beledian writes his poetry and prose in Western Armenian and publishes them through small printing presses in Los Angeles and Yerevan. Deliberately sidestepping the mandate for international marketability, his novels push language to new heights, to a form of aestheticization, uncompromised by demands for universal readership.

His fiction demonstrates a style that falls somewhere between those of the nouveau roman and the postmodern novel. He often shuns punctuation rules, sequential plot lines, and reliable narrators. Although his novelistic forms are overwhelmingly inspired by French post-structuralist thought, their linguistic acrobatics and content are strikingly representative of the post-1915 Armenian diaspora, marked like it by a sense of chronological interruption and geographic dispersion. His novels highlight language's performative capability, often oscillating between the dominant Western Armenian literary form and passages in Classical Armenian, Eastern Armenian, the Mush dialect, and colloquial Turkish-Armenian. In doing so, they raise two questions regarding aesthetics and representation: first, how does a catastrophe, an event that by its very nature defies meaning, find representation in language, a system of meaning-making; and second, what does it mean to represent a diasporic cultural experience in an infinitely exilic linguistic form?

In reflecting on these questions, Beledian proposes a theory of language and catastrophe that complicates the translation of his oeuvre. Even before translation, he sees a disjunction between language and content in contemporary Western Armenian literature, for the language of writing is no longer suited to a way of living. In other words, Western Armenian, which has survived only in diaspora settings since the 1915 genocide, has ceased to be the organizing logic of its inheritors' everyday encounters and interactions; it no longer dictates their mode of thought. Beledian's writings portray language as a performance of culture and depict its divorce from—its emptying of—people. Seen in this light, Western Armenian, as a literary language and not a living one, can no longer produce content. Its performance can only be self-referential, and therefore untranslatable.

"In the Language of Catastrophe" is the chilling and poetic account of the Armenian catastrophe as the un-peopling of a language.

Talar Chahinian

VEHANOUSH TEKIAN

"Forgive me for all those words"
"There will be silence in the museum   and phantom of death"
"To explain without words"
"The ruins call intensely   with their stubborn"

(poetry)

Translated by Karen Jallatyan

Forgive me for all those words

Forgive me for all those words
which I rudely relayed to you
forgive me for all those words
that I whispered to others softly
forgive me for the complicated immense moments
which I secretly gave you
for the brief and toneless days
which I gave to others openly
You are the half-finished cuneiform etching
                                        on the leaf of a palm tree
You are the plenitude of power of my times
which like Indian arrows
                        darted without a trace

It is the everyday feast,
Always unusual in our meeting
From this low and narrow bed of mine
I shall write lullabies on the walls of night
in order that with untroubled
                                    brittle sentiment
you come to me again
and with mortal sinful and reed-plaited
fingers I reveal your etching's new meaning
you sing the merry tune of your newly budded palm tree
you breathe my body
                        with wild words
like arrows that rise

translucent foam
to my blood's eruption

And you love again
and you forgive once more

**There will be silence in the museum
and phantom of death**

There will be silence in the museum   and phantom of
death
and delusion of
life
in the tranquility the past speaks mutely self-confident
as if the present does not exist   and the future even
in this present turns into past
museums reign with lights
But my museum is dark   noisy
like a sunset
like a street that neither ceases
nor petrifies
like an immense heart that can palpitate
with pure blood
like a memory that blunts
neither in pleasure
nor suffering
you are everywhere in my museum
And when I am here every moving thing becomes definite
voices break in   more intense
more binding and ungraspable
I turn the lights on
lights of words
lights of metal
lights of blood
What do you want from me? that under the colorless eye of
the lamp

one moment you are dead
one moment alive
from me what do you want? with the painful gaze of a cripple
you gaze around you

To explain without words

To explain without words
I used words
To relate without stumbling
I used a ladder
To cry out loud
I used laughter

Someone saw me crying
he has laid down now
I descended to his arms
and on the inexplicable
                                        nakedness
I drew the cover of words

On the palms of my hands he played with
Rene Magritte's three apples
Paul Klee's centrifugal letters
and Salvador Dali's self-absorbed
                                    third eye

I covered him too
with soul-searching smile
and with woman's densely-lit ambiguous advice
The rain went deeper into the night
                              the night became pregnant
                                   with voices

With domestic voices venomous unapproachable
that turn the soul violent
and then,
with bloodthirsty knives the three apples
gave me my unshut eye
and then,
I caressed the braille letters of life
and the gallop of the hands
was a wind-blown ciphered night
                                        on the dark pillow was born
this savage scintillating
                                                        femininity

The ruins call intensely with their stubborn

The ruins call intensely with their stubborn
gaze they bury all novelistic forms
they bury the epic the bread the wine the song the
drought
fertility the anthills multiply
under the sun live these strong-winded ruins
like an insoluble truth drop by drop they ooze their heart
to the earth while the breeze like a startled herd
passes from country to country as if a cursed legion far-off
the Eye hiding its sins submerges into the cerulean instability
to tell the rest of the myth the Eye opens
and millions of people drop by drop are descended to the
earth
the tribes multiply like fate
arranged side by side and absurdly tourniqueted

and we wait for somebody to murder the spies of pain

The problematic nature of translating poetry—of transposing formal and semantic configurations from one language to another, hoping to give an afterlife to a poem—already finds a deeply sensitive home in Vehanoush Tekian's poems, as they grapple with the flickers of meaning that envelop us from the un-patterned chaos of life. What better way, then, to honor the poet on the occasion of translating some of her poetry than by weaving a poem that is literally, formally and genetically attached to it?

Karen Jallatyan

CHRISTIAN BATIKIAN

"Winter Soldier"

(fiction)

Translated by Tamar Boyadjian

There is a strange nothingness. Bucky Barnes will always remain a young lad (*and no one stays dead . . . except Bucky*).[1]

2014 – And years later, Leo will return to his city. And when he exits the airport he will find himself in that ring of wandering and perpetually bohemian children, who stubbornly will yell *para, para, para.*[2] It is at this moment that Leo will realize that his decades of absence hadn't changed a thing in this city. Throwing some *kuruş*[3] at that unceasing laughter, those children hollering at him, he will hurry to shelter himself in the nearest taxi. Kadıköy,[4] he will say to the taxi driver, with his voice cracking.

Winter again, snow again.

Even as a child, Leo didn't like the winter; not even New Year's or his birthday at the end of January. He can't explain exactly why. Probably because he was a depressed child. But now he is nineteen years old, and he still doesn't like New Year's or his birthday. He still doesn't know. He is probably still depressed and hasn't realized it.

You could say it is not an easy thing being born in winter.

. . . that year it was so damn cold in Bolis, oğlum[5] *we haven't seen anything like this . . . Snow, snow everywhere . . . someone*

---

[1]A common joke that circulated in the comic world, "No one stays dead except Bucky." The reference here is to Bucky Barnes, a sidekick character in the *Captain America* comics which appeared in 1941 under Timely Comics, the predecessor of Marvel. Bucky was brought back several decades later as the "Winter Soldier," who for a short time assumes the role of Captain America when Steve Rogers (Captain America) was assumed to be dead.

[2]The Turkish word for "money."

[3]The Turkish word for monetary change, or cents.

[4]Kadıköy is the name of the most prominent and one of the largest cosmopolitan districts of Istanbul, Turkey. It faces the historic center of the European side of the Bosphorus, on the northern shore of the Sea of Marmara.

[5]The Turkish word for "son."

could be buried in it . . . the war on the other side . . . Uff! it was soo cold . . . everyday news came from the nursery that once again babies were dying from the cold . . . can you imagine . . . ?

No one had any hope he would live. You will die, they said; but he didn't. Two days later, they handed him over to his mother and sent them both home. An expressive child wrapped up in blankets, wailing instead of speaking.

. . . and your name, well; they called you something à la française . . . and I said it is lame, and if it wasn't for your mother they apparently would have killed the child . . . back then they were afraid of our names . . . they said, they can tell who you are from your name, and kill you . . . oh, and they didn't kill anyone; it is the cold that knows no race, no nation . . . but come and try to explain that here . . .

It was the same date. He was born, and Bucky got lost in the snow. He realized that, but it was too late. Now, it is January 1964, and once again it is freezing and winter all over Turkey. I mean a cold—they said for this kind of weather and every other such cold—the likes of which we have never seen in Bolis!

1964 – It's been ten days and there is a frightful cold in all of Turkey. Bolis, Smyrna and all of Anatolia is covered in snow. In Anatolia, numerous people have frozen to death. The produce, fruits and vegetables, all ruined. The famished wolves have reached the villages and towns.[6]

[6]These sections in the text dated 1964, which also report on the conditions of weather in Turkey, are direct references taken from the January 25, 1964 newspaper *Aztag*—a famous Armenian daily newspaper which is printed until today in Beirut, Lebanon.

A life entirely in white darkness. A murkiness that is not entirely murky. Perhaps they keep in that murkiness, those who would become gods. The lads, taken from their mothers and kept in that darkness, so then later they would be brought to the light for just one strike of the blade. After this, they would become gods.

Could it be that a somber light appeared white (white?) behind the membrane. In that life, there were no human voices, but he remembered, or perhaps he thought he remembered, a voice; a century ago (a lifetime ago?).

I'll always be with you Bucky

Was his name Steve? Something else? He didn't remember. Only, an airplane they were going to rescue from the nefarious ones, despite all obstacles. They said their victory depended on it. Then, a powerful explosion. Then, Steve (is he remembering his name correctly), his hand; him, as a last resort; and hanging from that hand, he oscillates from that brim.

Don't let me fall Steve I beg you

I'll always be with you Bucky

But his voice always betrayed him, and he let him fall from the plane. The descent was slow; he approached the ocean of white snow, he approached to later escape it. But only a soft fall at first and then plunging, until . . . did it last a day? perhaps a month . . . he can't remember where he came down.

And then one day—how many years or a century later—beyond the membrane, the light grew stronger. Bucky felt nothing, but the light began to stubbornly penetrate through the surface of the snow, and now he was forced to feel nothing. Then this sort of warm wetness occurred; drops of snow started running down his face from his temple, to his neck, his chest, further down. Little by little, he began to feel himself again, warmer than the surrounding snow. Then he realized he could move his legs. He likely stayed that way for a year; until one day, in the night, an aged wolf sniffed out Bucky. The wolf dug, and dug, until he reached a frozen face. A pair of ice-cold eyes began to gaze at him with a certain indifference, such that the beast suddenly felt this extreme disappointment. It is then that he remembered his youth, how the little girl had tied a red ribbon around his neck, and he was so proud. He remembered that he was not a wolf, rather a wretched dog, who being kicked out of his home had merely imagined himself as a powerful beast one day. At that point, he was disappointed; he realized the end was near and moved away. He didn't touch the boy; dogs are supposed to be loyal to humans, aren't they?

But Bucky's face remained that way, exposed. Insensibly, he took in the fresh air, but he had clearly lost the ability to breathe, his lungs ached immensely. In the morning, the sun ascended and hit him directly in the eyes; his body was protected and his eyes shut. It was this first movement in years. Two days later, he suddenly decided to move his legs. The snow was not falling down hard anymore, the membrane disintegrated; and he remained there lying; exposed. In the mornings, under the sun; in the evenings, against the wind. A month later, however, he felt that he craved the cold snow again. It was his first wish, after all this time. He didn't understand it either, how he got up from his place. His body had hardened—he fell; he got up; he fell again; he got up again, until he recovered the ability to move. Then he submitted his face to the wind, awakening his sense of smell to direct his walk towards the cold.

Two months later, and nineteen years after his fracture, Bucky Barnes reached the border of Turkey.

> 1964 - The oranges are ruined in Adana, Chorkmarzban,[7] Antioch, and Alexandretta. The farmers have set wood on fire to save the trees. The temperature has fallen to 15 below zero. Because of the excruciating cold, ten people have already died; it is only the 20th of the month; a pack of wolves have now reached the outskirts of Bolis.

. . . this winter is just too damn long . . .

And granny, from coughing and speaking to who knows who, has gotten up from the creaky footstool and walks towards the kitchen, swaying to and fro. Perhaps this was the same way the mother had walked from the nursery in the winter of 1945; alone.

. . . they enlisted your father in the army, and me . . . I had such a fever, I was coughing as though my lungs were going to overflow through my mouth . . . back then no one believed I could be up and about again . . . what was your mother to do? she had to come home with you, alone . . . what do I know? she probably caught a cold, or something must have happened at the hospital; in those years, anything could have happened . . .

---

[7]Originally in Armenian, Chorkmarzban, currently called Dörtyol in Turkish, is a port city located near the easternmost point of the Mediterranean coast, at the head of the Gulf of Iskenderun.

did you think it was easy bringing a child in this world in that cold? . . . in two, three weeks, wilting away, we never knew exactly how she died . . .

There is no electricity; the meager light of the candle glitters, alone. You must be insane to go out in this type of cold, but granny should not see the cigarette in hand.

The garden, frost bitten, but not deserted; the presence of another felt in the twinkle of an eye. Some time later when his eyes became accustomed to the darkness, the outline of the maimed body became apparent—a boy, standing alone, so alone that Leo was not afraid.

hey . . . hello! . . . merhaba . . . ahlan . . . [8]

No such sound or no movement; he came closer, a fixed stare.

Hello . . . ?

He suddenly spoke.

I speak English

His voice was cold; he exhaled the snow.

Who are you? What are you doing here?

I am Bucky. I came here, but it is really cold

It's not that cold, are you crazy?

Where I come from is much colder . . . it was good

Eh, why did you come then?

[8] Arabic salutation.

It wasn't cold anymore

Hmmm . . . you need the cold for some reason?

No, I just want it

You want a smoke?

Sure, give me one

It was then when he reached for the cigarette that Bucky realized that his left arm was not there; did it tear off during the fall . . . or perhaps before then?

What is this place?

Kadıköy . . . Istanbul . . .

Turkey? . . . what did you do after? which side did you end up? . . .

You who? . . . what side? . . .

I am talking about the war

What war?

What year are we in?

Are you kidding?

No

1964

Oh . . . only nineteen years . . . oh I thought it was longer . . . Any news from Steve? What is he up to?

Who's Steve?

Captain America

Huh? . . . what did you say your name was again?

Bucky . . . Bucky Barnes

Nah, you are teasing me!

No

Well, I think you are out of your mind

Leo turned around and stormed home out of anger.

2014 – The house is simply just not, but the garden is always the same. Leo will never realize the trees are different; but their house is on the other end of the block. And the outline of the corrupted body will not entangle itself into Leo's memories.

The next morning, he found no one in the garden, but thought about coming back out after going inside. He was there again.

Where were you this morning?

I was buried in the snow; that morning sunlight just killed my eyes

You hungry?

No

Did you have something to eat?

No, I don't eat

You are weird

Perhaps

Want a smoke?

Ya

So you think it isn't cold enough here?

No, I am too warm

That's not a good thing?

That's not a good thing

1964 – The wild boars and the wolves have attacked the region of Buragni.[9] A shepherd and his three hundred sheep have frozen to death. The temperature has fallen to 25 below zero in Sepastia; countless people are freezing.

So you are saying there is no news from Steve, huh?

No, it has been a long time maybe he is lost or dead I don't know

Hmmm

I am sorry

No problem

Were you close?

Likely . . . I don't know . . . I don't remember . . .

I think we were supposed to free the airplane and it exploded, right?

[9]Most likely a reference to the original Armenian name of one of the provinces of Turkey. Perhaps current day Bingöl in Eastern Turkey.

Maybe

You don't want to talk?

No

I think it was after that explosion you two were lost . . . they tried to find you but they couldn't

You know? In our day we didn't have these kinds of cigarettes

It's funny to hear you say "in our day," you look younger than me

Well, if you were buried under the snow for that long, you would look young too

2014 – The next day, Leo will try to find his childhood friends. It is then that he will realize his memory has gotten weak; neither a name nor a face; he can't remember. Leo will become worried; he is not even seventy yet; what happened?

I hadn't realized how granny had gotten closer.

Who . . . ? is this . . .

Uh . . . Bucky

Oh no! the poor boy doesn't have an arm, or any proper clothes . . . boy, do you have any sympathy! . . . in this cold . . . he will freeze and catch pneumonia . . .

Without seeking approval, she grabbed Bucky's only arm and dragged him towards the house.

Bucky was confused by the warmth of the house, but it

really wasn't that warm at all. The fireplace was merely preserving the memories of its heat. With great difficulty, Leo was able to convince his granny that she need not rekindle the fire.

He's used to the cold

You know . . . your friend seems a little off

Then from her fictitious hiding place, she suddenly took out some rose jam; god knows where she got her hands on it.

I shall make some tea now

No, I don't want it

I don't understand this language you speak, but if you say "no" one more time, I will pour the contents of this kettle all over your head

You understand?

Bucky understood.

With a worrisome face, Leo followed Bucky who sipped the hot tea with explicit disappointment.

oğlum[10] *you have a mother a father*

(says, do you have parents?)

My mother died when I was young . . . my father died during the war

(says, mother died when he was a çocuk[11] *and his father died during the war)*

---

[10]The Turkish word for "my son."
[11]The Turkish word for "child."

Oh no the çocuk is an orphan

Granny!

Well, if he is an orphan why shouldn't I say he is an orphan

Where do you come from, you say?

(asks where do you come from?)

The truth is I don't know . . . Germany or Austria . . . the snow melted and I came here

You came through the snow?

(Granny you understand English???)

Yes, I cut through the snow . . . it was difficult . . . I would plunge, get up, fall down, get up, walk . . .

We would walk that way in the desert . . . it was hard . . . we would push forward, fall, get up, fall down, get up, walk . . .

. . . The provinces of Austria or Germany . . . across those snowy fields

. . . Trebizond . . . across the seashores . . . the deserts

What are you two talking about?

Huh?

It is cold, let me restart the fire

1964 – Twenty-three kilometers from Dikranagerd, at the apex of Karajaghi, a military subunit of sixty men is stuck in the snow, and liberating forces have gone to their aid. In Mardin, due to the snowstorm, the windows have shattered and the chimneys have flown off in hundreds of homes in the city. The water pipes have burst and the power is out. In Uludali, the snow is two meters high. This is the second time in a hundred years that Lake Van has frozen from the cold. The Turkish papers report that Turkey has not seen this kind of impetuous winter in the last twenty years.

The winter doesn't seem so cold when you have such a crippled and helpless friend, who comes by every night to drink tea and eat rose jam with you. But in April, the cold will retreat, and after a long winter the people will count the dead and figure the damages. And the springtime will not arrive cheerfully. And once again you will be alone. And your comic hero friend will even go away.

2014 – A cold wave will pass from the stomach; the third day of visitation. And the key ring will fall from his hand. And the doorman will yell after him in vain, *efendi.*[12] While after every step, the aging Leo will approach with a staggering walk the posters of films. He will see the large banner, "Captain America: Winter Soldier." And everything will return, and it is as though granny is still alive and will serve tea with rose jam again.

He's leaving now.

Where will you go?

I don't know . . . I haven't decided yet . . . maybe I will look for Steve, or maybe walk

[12]A title in Turkish meaning "lord" or "master" and used to demonstrate respect, especially towards the elder. It comes from Greek, and in 20th century Turkish it functions like ma'am & sir, the gendered forms beyefendi and hanımefendi are in use instead of efendi, denoting respect, regardless of age.

towards Russia

Will we meet again?

Perhaps . . . I don't know

Bucky . . .

Yes

Um . . . take care of yourself

You too

This is how the friendship ends, when they let him fall from the plane, or when you decided to move away, searching for the cold.

It just simply ends.

2014 – The Emek movie theater in Yeşilçam is just the same. Winter again, snow again; you would say time was confused at a standstill again. Leo will exit the theater and search for his time. Then he will feel afraid. Then he will take a taxi. *Airport*, he will whisper to the driver. Leo will want to escape. Leo will not return to his room; he doesn't need his things. And the taxi will speed through the street of the old city. The streets are clothed differently; their names have changed. But they will always seem the same. As if the years had not passed over them. 1964 will be longer and longer. Until the end of time. Until the end of Leo's time.

There are words; then the remnants; then the memory.

Then, the words again: a surviving trace for the reader, a testimony to recollection, whose eyes cast the first translation, a part of which becomes imprinted to memory.

Then the translator, whose words serve another form of forgetting and remembering, a witness to a version and the mediator of another; here, a testimony to an Armenian original and its afterthought—to a cycle of loss and return.

The words and the story are lost, and rejuvenate themselves through the return of the new literary text, a language that is other than the original, but finds kinship through its desire to fulfill the same type of cultural memory. And in the spaces between the original and the translation remains a bursting silence, whose rebirth through the process of rewriting is like our character Leo: returning to his childhood home, returning to places only to find that the world around him has changed and remained the same, simultaneously; and the thread that connects him to his past, to the stories of old, is his story of Bucky Barnes, the Winter Soldier—in fact, a revenant of tales that are born again in a re-presence and re-turn, in storytelling and translation itself.

The self-reflexive nature of this text—including its fragmented structure, its repetition of words, and its intertextuality—reminds us that translation is not merely the attempt to transfer meaning from one word to another, but that it goes beyond language, beyond cities, beyond the notion of simply filling brackets with phrases; behind familiar and foreign *words lies the human condition, the kinship between the literary products of every culture.*

Tamar Boyadjian

ARA KAZANDJIAN

From *suspended line*

(poetry)

Translated by Aram Kouyoumjian

17

the frozen sadness of an
unmasked night
unmasked and ripe
akin to a love
hour by hour I enter within
line by line I too become frozen
there
where you grew to the stature
of my city
becoming as familiar with my soul
as my city is

line by line
I find you
—the night sings sadly
batting its weary eyes—
I extend my hand to you
playing the song of
encounter in your eyes

—destroyed—
that grew up tearless

it is you I now seek
even more than my city
to live within you

27

that which far away
we birth in silence
separates here from its core page by page
that which becomes an abode
a day lost within the year
remains my love
love

47

I came
but only after being lost
the road was empty
though dark,
I came having pocketed the darkness
crossing over the heart
I came
and found you
naked—city

39

eyes of darkness
shut
where I was born alone
barefoot outside the city
perhaps shivering,
there where the winds
spoke instead of singing

there where many others
forgot their birth
I
am not
contrary

45

as if
in the night of the dead city
we were born
with no way back
naked—
whimpering
we won't return there anymore
where
we don't know where
but here the trees of spring
are bare

we
naked—as if
our eyes naked
as the night
of the dead city

as if
you left me with the light
arrived afar

7

again
I embrace you with my destiny
we are together now—
my loneliness
it is your love
your loneliness my pain
I embrace you
together with the street
and we arrive
in the city
arm in arm
up the street—
down the street

from the café
we move on to the house
Rochechouart No. 61
where my uncle
has piled words
of intoxication
in lieu of tears

empty
like the streets of autumn
—I am now silent within—
my insides ashes of birth
as a picture
—my life has turned into an image of the past –

(there is no more sound from without
all sounds are asleep)

31

to be
after everything
always
night
and to sway with fortune
for the light

to be
with everything
always
dark
and to wait with hope
for the end

to be
in every country
at the same time
and to feel lonely
alone

In ancient city lamentations, the destruction of cities results from the departure of a protecting goddess, to whom female mourners negotiate the fate of their city and community. This select collection of poems from Kazandjian's latest book, suspended line, reflects the experience of a Diasporan Armenian, whose loneliness exists "in every country / at the same time." The lover, likened to the city itself, becomes the object of affection sought by the narrator as a place to "live within" and as a place of comfort. But that solace is temporary, and our narrator painfully embraces the lover, "together with the streets," silently moving through familiar places – spaces of the past which now are "all sound asleep." "In the night of the dead city / we were born" – the city was lost, just like the narrator who came upon her. The protective goddess has departed, leaving her city bare and naked, void of light, a place where the winds cease to sing. But these poems attempt to revoke this befallen fate where, "many others / forgot their birth." Unmasked, through these suspended lines, they sing a lament of their fate through poetic verses.

Tamar Boyadjian

ANI ASATRYAN

"Words"

(fiction)

Translated by Narine Jallatyan

It is enough that you close your
eyes and repeat in your head,
one time, with words, that your
father has not died; it is so, that
the deceased is not your father.

I begin my experimental essay. Writing only becomes possible after an event. The time of words is always the after something. To write one has to have the irresistible ability to realize objects and phenomena in words: a capacity to actualize the world within words, to make yourself real in words.

1

Being able to complete something had become an obsession. Always, when (*she has forgotten the word*) she is on the threshold of being realized, she turns her back. She would walk from one corner of the room to the other, from one to the other, from one to the other, counting the months left until completion.

Completion?

A finish?

A halt?

In her head, a thousand times she replayed, in detail, the image of the series of days, which had followed one another incessantly for two years already. The same day was constantly repeating itself. If nothing happened for another few months, she could finish her studies.

To finish?

To complete?

Then, she would be deprived of the opportunity to turn this phase of her life into a story of words.

To be deprived?

In vain?

Vain?

After a two-year interruption, she once again felt the power that suppresses that irresistible ability, the one that had surfaced and demanded to be realized.

In the evening, after two bottles of beer, she told her boyfriend of her intention to quit. The next day she regretted expressing her thoughts in **words**. Now she was certain that, again, nothing would (*she has forgotten the word*). She would be walking from one corner of the room to the other trying to recall the conversation from yesterday **word** for **word**. At least she was hoping she had spoken her mind with the wrong **words**.[1]

2

The indomitable desire to leave things half complete had arisen yet again. Right after his departure. During the summer they had lived together (which quickly passed) she had

[1]Word—Phantasm (Modern Armenian Expository Dictionary, Edward Aghayan, "Armenia," Yerevan, 1976).

not written a word. They had met over the winter. At first everything went smoothly. The idea for the story had emerged from a brief conversation on a mundane topic. While speaking of different things they had both uttered the "**real**" word, and subsequently something important changed. On her way home she was thinking of this emerging relationship with words characterized as "**real.**" For the first time words were yielding to reality, which [reality] had been given the definition of the "**real**." She could not find a way to think of the occurrence in words, because it had already been defined as "**real**." Reality was no longer a fabric of words. It was **real**.

During the entire summer (which quickly passed) the desire to leave anything half complete had not yet emerged. The wish to replace reality with words had turned itself on its head. Words—which were more in number than the flowing days and seconds of that quick summer—were being uttered for the one and only purpose of **re-al-i-za-tion**. To leave stories unfinished in the most interesting places and replace them with words had yielded to the crazy impulse of realizing all stories written in words. **Desire**. The image of the billboard having momentarily caught her eye in the morning was realized entirely on the evening of the same day. Any new idea, even if it was the most abstract; every text she read, from the philosophical to journalistic; a fleeting musical phrase that she heard, an image from the novel turned into film, or a poetic syllable that could occupy her mind were realized into stories a few hours later. Words, sounds, feelings, thoughts, images, letters, lines, everything was disentangling itself from the pressure of being pleasurably realized.

Words especially. **Words**. Under the influence of that power devouring all and everything with the speed of light, words had acquired an equivalent place in reality. Every uttered word was immediately turning into either an object or an act. It seemed as though the rhythm that had filled everything with the irregular flow of a wave, and had turned time into a course, was ceaseless. The **Rhythm**. Over time she had expelled words, hoping that at least this time reality would not recoil in the face of them. Now in this drawn-out winter outside, and the unreal distance which divides the two of them again, words pretend to replace the world.

3

She was little when she discovered the magical power of recreating reality in words, and of possessing the world with words. On the way to school,[2] closing her eyes tightly, she had repeated in her mind, with words: "**father has not died, father has not died, father has not died,**" and the deceased was no longer her father. With that self-confidence, common to children, she had begun to experiment with this newly discovered magical skill everywhere. After a short while, all of her friends were convinced she was living in an antique summer house full of servants, in a perfectly happy family. She too was convinced of this. Even more so. She **could** close her eyes for a moment and repeat with words anything that came to her mind, and reality would transform into these words, words

[2]In school her name was Helen Smith. She had lost her memory: how old she was then or what year she started school. But if her name was Helen Smith at that time, then she must have been born in 1861. Therefore, it was in the 1870s that she went to school.

that she had uttered in her head. Through time she adopted the most distinctive of magical skills. Then she began to live in a place where everything was covered in words. Even the cement and the reinforced concrete of huge architectural structures were made of words. She had also mastered the skill of recreating the reality of others in words. This was a real discovery, a magical ability more attractive than any childish game. Like tin soldiers, she had begun to transport people she knew, one by one, to that swaying space of words. From typical apartments, she had transported her teachers to huge, bright summerhouses; she had liberated them from worrying so they could write their important examinations without needing anything. This much had not satisfied her. She had become so sophisticated that, at one point, she had even read one of her teacher's papers, then the other, and another. She had left a couple for later. To her friends, she had given surnames of universal importance and had overseen every step they took. They had to fit their newly appointed calling. If not, she would again close her eyes, and repeat in her head (with words), that those with the new surnames were her friends, and those with the new surnames would be her friends. Again, reality was plummeting.

4

She knew nothing about his days. To know nothing, one must do something: to break off contact with those who knew how to make stories of words about him. Them, especially. Distance was the possibility of her words. She had burdened that period of time so much with layers of words that later, (after two decades) when she made an attempt to remember the prehistory, she had found that words had placed such a dense layer upon reality that circumventing them would already become someone else's life. Never again had she made such an attempt. The erased **memory** had been definitively replaced by the **memory** of words. She had forgotten everybody who could bear witness to other kinds of **memory**.[3] Every time she met someone she had forgotten, she was amazed that the stranger had recognized her.

5

The presence of words everywhere was necessary for her existence. She doubted her existence wherever words did not exercise sovereignty. In the beginning, sometimes, but later even more: she would always be forced to recoil, to make her existence in words possible. To leave everything **incomplete** was perhaps her only rule. To protect. Words. Now that it was this drawn-out winter outside, again, the desire to yield to the irresistible sovereignty of words had risen in revolt. This time, her education was to remain **incomplete**. She was looking for the proper words to turn the business of leaving things **incomplete** into a story. Perhaps not finishing things is the only way to give space to words. Any relationship, action, and story that could become whole and ended in silence—was a threat to

[3]Memories: materials that carry genetically foreign information for the organism and generate a specific immune response upon entering the organism through antibodies and t-lymphocytes. "Memories" are all those materials which when entering the organism are recognized by the immune system as foreign and induce the formation of an immune response.

words. Just like when the last gunshot was to be fired as she was leaving home, the hand had shaken. If the gunshot had rung, the way all the gunshots of the world ring: “bang-bang,” she would be deprived of the possibility to realize the ending of the story in words. So then she had closed her eyes a thousand times and had thought of a thousand melodic variations of that gunshot. Just like when she found herself upon a romantic relationship (those always remained up in the air); afterwards her guys or girls would stand—confused and ridiculous—in front of one another, a vision of words, the story unfamiliar to their own stories—unregimented. Her masterfully synthesized vision of words was to acquire absolute power over reality; and reality was plummeting again.

6

She had gotten used to it already—that when reality, like a herd of horses, revolts in the face of wordy textures, there needs to be distance in order for words to restore their power. And she would distance herself to cultivate new forms and syntheses of words. Maybe in an island. No. In her four-walled cubicle. Well, ya, it is the same as an island.

* * *

Upon completing the history course with (high) honors during her first year at the university,[4] she had decided to work

[4]In university, her name was Helen Keller. She had lost her memory: how old she was then or what year she started the university. But if her name was Helen Keller at that time, then she must have been born in 1880. Therefore, it was in the 1900s that she was a university student.

not towards the development of her memory, but the contrary. Enemies live inside memory. She was obsessed with making sure that historical events, dates, and people's names would occupy the memory she was saving with care, for words. It was necessary to remember everything only temporarily. To learn; then completely forget it. She was reading the books of her favorite authors in this way. What is read must be forgotten immediately, so that one can write it again using different words.[5] Thus, memory was constantly being subjected to a violent unloading. She had perfected this technique to the point that she had the power to completely forget the next day whatever happened to her the day before. That emptied space emerging in her memory was a carefully opened space meant for words. It was necessary to forget everything in order to allow for the possibility of re-writing in words. So, she was forced to learn how to forget to build another memory of reality.

7

She does not remember section seven of the text.

[5]One writes: "Sometimes, the author writes with a fixed program conceived in advance, attempting to find solution to the question she put forth and to develop the storyline when, suddenly, she departs from the route. Probably, a fresh thought, or another image, or a whole new subplot has come to her mind. If you ask what conditioned this digression, she will not be able to answer. It can be that she did not even notice the change, even though she is now producing a completely fresh material, and, apparently, previously unknown to her. However, at times it is possible to show convincingly that what she has written resembles, in obvious ways, the work of another author; a work she thinks she has never even seen."

8

(*she cannot remember the word*) she had gotten to a place where the game had the pretense of turning into reality. She had the feeling it was no longer herself synthesizing the textures of words; now they were forcing her to adjust to their syntheses. She failed to find any principle at the basis of syntheses. They were arbitrary. Once a seemingly magical skill had now been put into work like an engine and operated ceaselessly. In the past—to influence reality—she would shut herself in for days to find the unique syntheses of words. Now, in a second, words were arbitrarily lining up next to each other without any necessity for synthesis.

9

The obsession of forgetting everything

Snip

The nostalgia for the word

Snip

glades ruptures empty places

Snip

Naught and light muddy foamy light weightless naught and light

10

The ability to realize the world with words had reached its limits over the winter. The obsession of leaving stories unfinished, in order to complete them in words, had recoiled. Instead, she had begun to feel satisfied in making stories of invented events. Words had established their total sovereignty. (*she cannot not remember the word*) there was no need to undertake anything. The mere telling of any story was enough. In the same way, after two bottles of beer, she had told her boyfriend she intends to leave her studies unfinished. It was enough that she had explained her intention in words. (*she cannot remember the word*) when she said it, she had already left her studies unfinished. Without closing her eyes, she had said it out loud: "I have an intention to leave my studies unfinished." And her studies had been discontinued. On Monday, wearing the shoes he gave her as a gift, she had gone to class assured that her studies had been left unfinished.

***

Words, like horses, had revolted on their hind legs, refusing to continue reality and to edit real stories. They had the ability to replace reality. It is not as if the world was finding continuity in dictionaries; the world was beginning and ending exclusively in dictionaries.

P.S. The above text has been made of 1,821 intervals and of the arbitrary synthesis of 1,844 arbitrary words, including the postscript.

A work of translation is finished, and yet it never really feels complete. Just like in the story below, nothing is complete or whole. Words occupy the space to transform an idea into a linguistic reality. Translation never feels complete. There could always be "other words" to re-create one linguistic reality in the space of another language. While the speaker of this story ponders the nature of the connection between language and reality, the translator works exclusively in the realm of a form of linguistic reality, transferring one linguistic texture into another, while never treating the transferred material as mere "information." In other words . . .

In other words, to translate is to delve into the infinite possibilities of being. Similar to writing, the translation brings the awareness that there is no one way of putting a sentence together or of translating a phrase, since the possibilities are infinite—a process which could bring the translator to a deadlock, succumbing to language that behaves like a nomad, never wanting to settle down. This infinite possibility of translation, then, invites the translator to be open and welcoming in spite of the risk of being carried away by them. There is also an impasse: with too many paths to take, one is petrified and unable to move. For we know language is flesh without bones, as the Armenian saying goes, լեզուն ոսկոր չունի*: it is flexible, plastic, and malleable.*

The puzzle of a translated text is complete, the last piece is in its place, and yet the translated work as a whole is not perceived as finished. It is never complete. However, in translation something is also gained. Just like Asatryan's story reflects, unwritten time is, in a way, wasted time; the reality, which has not been turned into a linguistic texture, is not really "real." Through transla-

tion, the text gains another linguistic reality; and, though different from the original, the translated text extends its existence. Because the imagination of both the text and the translator comes into play, the translator seems to have drawn limits to the infinite, to settle meaning that behaves like a nomad, while always engaged in a process of (re)creation through the exercise of the imagination.

The translation of this piece has afforded me, as the translator, the quite useful exercise of contemplating the way we treat language—a language we assume we "know" that still remains foreign. It is this critical positionality afforded by translation that allows for the exposure of what can easily go unnoticed in a language that remains native and foreign at the same time.

Narine Jallatyan

SHUSHAN AVAGYAN

"Blackselves"

(cross-genre)

Translated by Milena Abrahamyan with an accompanying essay by the Author

Blackselves[1†]

Without another word the women left us,
taking the taper with them and locking the door.
Through the long night we waited—for what we did not know.
—from Aurora Mardiganian's testimony, 1917

You probably won't jump with joy, my dear, if I start writing about myself. If I don't put pen to paper, I will forget. But before I do that, let me summarize what I would have liked to write and didn't. Today I was reading Platonov's *Dzhan* in English.

It's hard for me to start something new. At first I feel perplexed and begin to distort old sayings.

Say, the harsher the censor tries to silence a piece of writing, the more the reader is drawn to the text. But being drawn to something is rarely the same as grasping or comprehending it.

Here I was going to reflect on why everyone would be incapable of understanding the relevance (modernity) of S. Kurghinian today, and why *Lone Woman* has still not found its audience. I should have also written about the general disinterest and ignorance of Armenian women, and how they have lost themselves in the (hi)stories of others and given in to forgetting those writings, which are addressed to them. But Lara, this has already been discussed.

[1†] *Blackselves* is the original translation of the author for the title of this text. Although originally the translator found this English title to be problematic, since in English the word carries a different cultural weight from the Armenian, the translator respects the author's wish to maintain her original translation of the title. Alternative titles offered by the translator include: *Draftselves* or simply *Sevamenq*, an English transliteration of the Armenian neologism.

One of the most important things in art is to situate the objects, which have already been situated a thousand times before by others, correctly. Yet, what do we mean when we say "correctly"? Artsvi was asking yesterday (once again) whether it is really easier to translate from English to Armenian, but I have already addressed the question of why it is easier (for me) to work from Armenian to English in my first book, Artsvi: I am trying to understand myself in a foreign environment. I think it was Bakhtin who wrote that identity becomes even more real and conceivable in a milieu of "foreignness," during the (imperative) process of being made foreign.

Maya Deren's short films of the 1940s. A black and white photograph: my grand mother with her wide brimmed hat.

The other day, I said that I won't let you cry, my dear, I won't tolerate your tears (externalized grief). To write every day; write every day. Remember when I was reading Celan's "Todesfuge" out loud?

"Black milk of daybreak we drink it at sundown, drink it at noon / in the morning we drink it at night / drink and drink . . . / Your golden hair Margarete / your ashen hair Shulamith."

But who wants to take the shortcut? Shortcuts are a misconception. A true work of words does not fly under any flag, it exists for itself.

Cultural trauma is even more unbearable, since—being deprived of reality—memory preserves the Terror of someone else's life and appropriates it.

Nika Shek's film about women football players, which, in

essence, is not about football. My grand mother says that I will never understand her pain, dark half-moons beneath her eyes. How to counter(situate)act the words so that the piece would become a poem.

Maya Deren returns to New York from Geneva and begins to research African voodoo dances. Buys a 16mm Bolex photo camera with money inherited from her father and films her most famous work, *Meshes of the Afternoon*, in 1943.

Rhythm alludes to life's bizarre existence. I keep thinking of Yerevan with its narrow alleys and neat four-story buildings. An intermediate passage.

We are testing in this book the possibilities of writing the self where the "inter-dimensional" and the "periodical" meet.

Or rather, we are counter-writing anything that may accidentally cause a misconception. If you don't understand one of our languages, find a translator.

I write every day; I am discontented with my writing every day. Valentina Calzolari said that she is in Yerevan and would like to meet, "I am grateful beyond measure for your novel," and so forth. I am paging through Stein's *A Novel of Thank You* at St. Mark's bookstore in Manhattan. This time the city seems more solemn, even familiar.

According to the project, each of us will write in the language in which we express ourselves with ease. Or the opposite, each of us will write in a language, through the difficulty of which we will articulate simple thoughts, which perhaps require a new evaluation. Or to put it in easier terms, the book that we are writing is founded on metonymy, a structure whereby names find substitutive meanings—each section is presented as an entirety.

My respected compatriots! Please let me return to Yerevan, arm in arm with Sarah, I want to—

Let me start again.

Rhythm alludes to life's bizarre existence. I keep thinking of Yerevan with its narrow alleys and neat four-story buildings. An intermediate passage.

On my round table lie the book *Unclaimed Experience: Trauma, Narrative, and History*, green Orbit chewing gum, keys, an empty beer bottle, a photograph of Djuna Barnes, and "a thousand and one trifles."

This arrangement, which seems utterly provisional or inconsistent, may be considered one of the main principles of a work of words: to counter(situate)act existing things in such a way so as to create new relational connections, imaginary associations, and versions of riddles that have numerous solutions.

I had expressed a wish in *Book-Untitled* with the hope that it would be read by our daughters, who would maybe show some curiosity regarding their past, but "maybe" is a relative word. Maybe, says Nancy, there is no connection between us. How can we create that relative connection, how can we appropriate a language that separates us?

Let's leave the classroom and see what's happening outside the academia, perhaps even on this very page. Do I contradict myself, Artsvi, when I say that it is easier to feel the earnest cadence of Armenian over the monotonous rhythm of English? Here once again I must highlight the need and importance of translational work, but not in technical terms. We must all become our life's translators and through comparison, deconstruction and resignification, we must find a new relational pattern or structure. Maybe this is the purpose of our book?

Once again I am patiently looking for a just approach; I am traveling without a map. It's imperative to decide which direction to take in order to get there.

When Kaputikyan writes in her famous poem, that it's possible to forget the mother, but it's impossible to forget the mother tongue, she contradicts herself, since "mother tongue" signifies that which comes from the mother.

Nancy writes (September 14, 2006) that the Utopiana seminars have been restarted and that the debates on post-Soviet Armenia are ongoing.

A photograph of Lake Van hangs on one of the walls in her living room. My grand mother with her foresight. I should have written about silence here, about how my grand mother would weigh each word, and, bending from their weight, how she had transformed into a scale. But first let me write about why this section of the book is called "Blackselves."

Gayane Chebotaryan was also a descendent of Armenians from Rostov-on-Don. She was born in 1918, received her degree in piano from the Leningrad Conservatory in 1943 (under

Kushnaryan). She composed a symphony titled "Celebration" (1945) for the Yerevan orchestra and choir on the occasion of the end of World War II. She also wrote the cantata "Armenia" (1947) for orchestra and choir, and from 1948 taught at the Yerevan Conservatory.

I have often been interested in disrupting the kind of mentality that lacks the capacity for critical analysis. In other words, the kind of mentality that originates from a narrow source.

In a dream my grand mother is walking fast through a narrow street and I am following behind. I am trying to catch up with her, calling for her to stop, but she does not turn and continues to walk. When my grand mother finally stops and turns toward me, her face is a mirror instead of a face.

What do we understand when we say "post-Soviet reality"? Every Tuesday, at nine in the morning, the woman with dyed hair comes to clean your apartment, but you never see her. She always walks on the tips of her toes. Once upon a time she was a dance teacher, but what does "once upon a time" mean?

The critics think without a doubt that they are doing us a favor by explaining, clarifying and discovering—or believing that they are discovering—our rough black drafts. He knocked, opened the door halfway and asked: "Will you have some coffee?" . . . and I lost my train of thought again.

I open the first page of Marcom's *The Daydreaming Boy* and read: "We are naked like Adam and the blue wide band now becomes what it is, the long sea rises before us, the notfish become what they too are, so that we see: water; white-capped waves stretched out into infinity; but not salt, warm, sad."

In her book, "we" signifies people without childhood.

In this book, "we" means something else. Although who's to say that these blackwords (draftwords) wish to be clarified? Critics still don't know how to approach Marcom's book, from which side to open it, from which page to start reading. James Barton's thick manuscript has not yet appeared on their desks, where on page 225 they can find the story of a four- or five-year-old girl who was found in 1918 in one of Syria's streets. When they attempt to clarify who she is in the orphanage, she has no answer. She doesn't understand Armenian at all and only when she is asked in Armenian "Who is your mother?" does she flinch at the word "mother" and her eyes come alive for a moment.

In Marcom's book this fragment appears on page 182 with very few changes. Almost everything is repeated, but in the new context descriptions become re-signified, everything is understood in a new way.

Our book poses a question. How can "we" reconceive ourselves in this blackafflicted body?

In her last years my grand mother was only sixty-one kilograms. Sixty-one kilograms of grief.

In the process of denial the denier eliminates various parts of the original and replaces them with newly formulated scripts. In other words, the movements of the ossified fingers change.

To write so that everything becomes unfamiliar, unalive. In other words, to kill off the words and sentences. Or like this: there is no passion, not today and not tomorrow. I am sad, Lara, tie your shoes, take your bag, come to me.

Hip-hop music: sweaty faces: smoke: I take out the bottle of beer from my breast pocket and (quickly) take a sip. He approaches me, extends his hand and says: Peace. And something bubbles up, swells, and explodes in my throat almost like a laugh, (peace for what?) and then Frenchie (Céline) approaches and saves me from a tactless situation.

Adapt, change your clothes: get in drag.

I am editing "our" life with its torn desires. Nancy, your face—like a half moon—is sometimes inaccessible to me, sometimes dark and unbearable.

In yesterday's dream three breastless women with long thick hair sit perched around something, howling and scratching out their eyes with their fingernails. Or maybe three priests, wrapped in their capes, whisper long prayers in almost feminine voices, singing, weeping, mourning. There they coerce blackus to occupy unmemoried spaces (to lead an inexplicable existence). Here, drunk with reality, Beyazit stands in front of me, frozen, as it were, with his hand hanging in the air.

My translations don't contain random words.

Step by step we begin to understand not only our everyday lives and activities, but the meaning behind the structure of this book, the reasons for its unity and motivations.

Last autumn when they expelled us from the Yerevan State University building, where we had a room with a small window filled with books and copies of the journal *Kanayq hayots*, Lara moved everything to the small apartment on Tumanyan street. It was cold, the boxes of books were heavy. The new center was almost like her fourth child: she would carefully take the books out of the boxes and in the same manner of care situate them on the new shelves. Those were probably the same bookshelves that held her unfinished comparative work on Zabel Yesayan and George Sand.

First of all, it is important to clarify how we understand the word "we," and then, what we attempt to do with that "we" in this book. How do "we" relate with one another, what are the connecting/unifying elements and what are the preventing/separating ones. It is imperative to read the three of us at the same time, in three different languages, in different voices and in different rooms, much in the same way as we are working on the book's construction right now. I don't read French, Nancy is not familiar with Soviet mores, Lara is not yet disappointed with this life.

It is important to understand the conditions allowing for the existence of three extreme views side by side, how differences can be constitutive of an integral unity.

I am running after my grand mother . . . I want to, I try to, impatiently, an awful need, this desire. I must see her face, but she disappears behind the arched wall.

In a monologue one person speaks and the rest listen/are silent. No new perspective or thought is created as a result.

In a polylogue several persons speak at the same time, argue with one another, explain and discover, reveal and become revealed.

Before knowing or having any idea about her own book, Marcom had opened Andranik Zarukian's memoir—not unintentionally, of course—and read the part about Boghos on page 31, which describes in detail the disciplinary work and punishments taking place in the orphanage. Here is a small excerpt:

> Every morning before being picked up from the floor, the beds would undergo a thorough scrutiny. Those who had wet the bed were separated and subjected to a variety of punishments. A first offender would be deprived of breakfast. If the offense was repeated, he would be denied food all day. At night, the wretch would be sent to bed with a public beating. (*Men Without Childhood*)

We are writing in order to understand the meaning of "we."

In his book James Barton views the disciplinary work of the orphanages as something positive. He believes that discipline returns orphans to a "normal life." In Marcom's book Vahé is not able to return at all. The elemental question is: a return to where?

Laws try to "disappear" us, silence and constrain us, but we continue to blackwrite, excavate and experiment.

Dionne Haroutunian writes in her letters that she has always been interested in questions of loss, recovery and integration. One of her works is titled *Self-Portrait During World War I*.

In the forefront of the print is a figure. It is unclear whether it's a figure of a woman or a man—it is actually an outline of a figure presented in an utterly strange, unnatural position, almost as if caught in the moment of falling backwards.

The posture of the hands is constrained and helpless. They are just as unbearable as the hands in Egon Schiele's numerous self-portraits: the long and thin fingers in the moment of stretching the tendons in such a way it seems they will never find a natural position, that they will instead stay that way for years and lifetimes evermore, almost as if paralyzed.

In the background is the field, black and dark red, having almost no depth, or rather, the contextual texture consumes, almost swallows the shrinking body.

Beyazit's sweaty hand. Hanging in mid-air.

And besides, they knew very little about psychological trauma during World War I and only after the catastrophe, in military hospitals, in Freud's notebooks did the terms and explanations, symptoms and etiologies gradually appear. Clearly Barton was unaware, he didn't know about all this, he was only a missionary, but he was one of the first people who was faced with and had to deal with the traumatic memories of those who survived. This was one of the main discoveries of Marcom's book.

Vahé's notmemory, his illegitimacy—his story is about those born in the harems (there were so many of them, did you know?).

I am eight years old and I am not yet a skilled reader, my grand mother's library is unattainable for me (literally, the cabinet is much too high for my height, built into the wall, a glass drawer for books rests upon a cabinet with wide wooden doors) and extremely tempting.

On Saturdays my parents always take me to her house to stay the night, and in the evening when she and my grand father watch television together I carefully approach the cabinet armed with a chair and select a book based on the color of its cover. Then I get down and hide (enter the/a moment) behind the wide doors in the middle, light a candle and with my heart racing, I open the book.

My grand mother is a doctor and many of her books contain descriptions of diseases, images of misshapen bodies, enlarged microscopic bacteria. This time I accidentally choose a thin book with a blue cover where there are almost no pictures.

After flipping through the pages for a while I finally find one black and white photograph in which people wearing plain nightgowns are laying down side by side.

The two in the foreground seem to be sleeping: the father holding his three or four year old child in his left arm, but I don't know why they are laying on the ground without a pillow or cover.

There are men in uniform standing next to them.

Without understanding, but with an uncanny feeling, I close the book and return it back to its place. This becomes my secret. Every Saturday evening, with the punctuality of a ritual, I take out the book with the blue cover for my "reading hour" and examine its only photograph.

There are no words in *Meshes of the Afternoon*; it seems as if the woman passes from one dream to another, as if trapped in the meshes.

But here is another established fact: censors will attempt to eradicate, while some of us will persist in our interest and discovery.

Later, when I was finally (impatiently) able to read (tracing every word with my index finger) the caption beneath the photograph, I never opened the book with the blue cover again.

Upon reading Marcom's book my students ask, how could Vahé recover his loss when the mairigs of the orphanage tried to fix everything with beatings and water? What about the tongue, speech, expression, what about the mind that constantly asks questions, what about language with its healing capacities, isn't it called "mother tongue" after all?

Loss feeds on silence.

Even your hand, Beyazit, hanging in mid-air, at this moment, years and lifetimes past, has no meaning, has already lost its capacity to heal.

I come from a culture of mourning, I don't know how to mourn. Instead—through incoherent details—I try to complete my grand mother's story, which I never got to know fully.

Let's get back to this book's construction and how we are attempting to create a unity full of differences, which should express the complex internal world of our relations. Today is a day of repetitions.

There are books, which you can accidentally lose or put under flowerpots, and do it not out of negligence. But there are books, the publication of which (also existence of the manuscript) is a joyful occasion, and among those is Mariam Tumanyan's concise (414-page) biography.

Here I would have liked to write about Artsvi's unusual effort and how he discovered Mariam Tumanyan, who of course has nothing to do with Hovhannes Tumanyan. I didn't write about it not because it's not an important topic or that I am not interested in it, but simply because it will distract us from our purpose. Besides, let me give others the chance to have something to write about.

Seventy years later, the Melkonian Educational Institute, which had opened its doors in 1926 for orphans like Vahé, continues to train generations of Armenians (with almost the same methods) each morning, standing in line in front of the central building, with the song "Aravod Luso," monotonous, our voices echoing those who came before us.

On one of those mornings when I couldn't get out of the bathroom, when everyone was already standing outside of the building, each class in its own row, and I was standing under the flow of cold water, that song transformed into something else in my ear: I was hearing my grand mother's voice, the flapping of black wings and "I've come to take you away with me."

Lara says that in order to live a woman must first kill her parents. She says it right here, in these pages, and I repeat: in order to live I tore her black wings and nailed them firmly to my shoulders.

One of the students says that the difficulty of the book results from the fact that it lacks a chronological sequence. It seems the text is woven around elements of repetition and fragmentation, and the act of reading itself transforms into a traumatic experience of comprehension.

The entire plot is revealed at the beginning of the novel, and throughout the novel the plot is deconstructed and reconstructed in a number of ways. The reader is barely able to hold onto any thread and follow the plot, when Marcom suddenly diverges from the storyline and begins a new version. The versions complete one another; each version is a whole.

Here is yet another version: my grand mother's father was a military blacksmith in Van. In 1915 they moved to Armenia with the Russian troops.

Marcom speaks on Vahé's behalf when she says: I would have liked to know what I don't know: the fact that I don't know my own Terror makes me even more terrible.

The unwelcoming walls of the Melkonian Institute and us standing beneath those walls, wearing our blue uniforms and black ties. Every night at ten o'clock Ms. Bekarian comes to check the cleanliness and orderliness of the rooms, probably in the same way Vahé's mairigs did, and if she doesn't like something she confiscates the ward's monthly pass to the city.

Marcom's book is a translation of men without childhood, or let me say it like this: it is the repetition of the same story but with another structure, with another syntax.

Vahé is waiting for his mother, he writes letters from the orphanage; the man without childhood escapes from his mother to an orphanage; two different boys from the same mother, or the same boy from two different mothers; the only things that are essential are the sea and the weather, the change in weather and the repetition, stability, return of the faithful waves (that is—grief).

Zarukian's book desires to end in anticipation, on the sea shore: "After the cruel grounds of the orphanages, where my childhood faded, and against the life opening in front of me, into which I projected my first step, that small notebook wrecked the blue sky of optimism, the love and faith and hope of which I had kept inside of me, even on the most depressing and cold days in the orphanage, just as a prisoner would longingly dream of a peaceful place, which awaits him inside the sweet promise of a free life . . ." Here the splash of the waves consumes the reflections of the man without childhood and Vahé's nightmare begins.

The book of the man without childhood is unfinished. Marcom attempts to finish it with another book, and that's her mistake. She becomes aware of this, but too late, since she discovers only in the process of writing that the book may come to an end, but it does not have a closure. In more than two hundred pages she tries to return, to understand, to find—that is, to find some closure—but she is unable to, or rather, it is impossible.

What I was going to write about and didn't: about Marc Nichanian's anti-critique and how I found myself in-between literature. I didn't write about Nancy, about Lara, and about myself. About how we would meet every Tuesday and talk about the structure of this book in a small room where the walls are painted an indescribable color.

If we are repeating one another it means that this book has reached its goal.

As punishment for not speaking in Armenian, Mairig would teach Vahé obedience, one blow after another with a rod; for speaking in this language the Zaptieh would silence Vahé's mother in a dark cellar through the use of violent force, but this language did not submit to any disciplinary measures, and this is what Marcom is showing in her book, in her not-words and notsentences, that Vahé's godlessness should not have been resolved through the rod, that the wound of the tongue, the disruption, the severance of language should not have been healed through blood-letting, but only through care, letter by letter, word by word, by studying, (exa)mining, understanding, translating.

Each of our different inquiries demonstrates one thing: the error of imagining and representing Armenian women in a singular way, that is to say, the error of simplification.

I wanted to write about Beyazit, about how he was trying to shake my hand in a bar one day, and how I was unable to, how my herculean strength would not give in, how I had frozen and become inert, otherwise I would not have ignored the gesture and would have wholeheartedly reached toward his extended hand.

I was also going to write an exercise-like dialogue where the speakers, the critics Hovig Tchalian and Ara Oshagan, would speak on the topic of Marcom's novel. Of course we know that such a thing exists, such a dialogue has already taken place, only in my imaginary meeting the critics would have a serious discussion and Hovig Tchalian would not repeat himself incessantly in the three pages assigned to him: "I found the novel's style instead to be for the most part contrived and too deliberate, far too involved in its own sense of experimentation," and Ara Oshagan would not interject: "For some books, the writing is done for the writing, not for the reading." But it's already too late, we have already reached the publishing house and besides, editors don't like changes.

I repeat and without irony that Marcom's novel does not merely bring to the fore psychological or historical themes (already discussed a multitude of times), but that this is where the language of the man without childhood is deconstructed, where the mother tongue is broken down. One comes to a very important realization: there is no return; it is pointless.

But I have once more strayed from the topic at hand, and this time irretrievably so. Forgive me.

On Blackselves

When I was asked to translate a piece for Absinthe, *accompanied by a short introduction that focused on the mechanics of translation, I proposed to do something else instead: to submit one of my own texts, "Sevamenq," and to write a commentary on the text and its translatability, or perhaps a postscript about deficit. The deficit of faithful translations of Armenian literature in English, the deficit of interest in translation in general in the English-speaking parts of the world, and more abstractly, the deficit of originals and the voids of meaning that are filled in with simulacral effects, as in the case of Aurora Mardiganian's testimony. So I come to this journal both as a writer and translator, more as a writer who has learned how to write by translating other writers.*

"Blackselves" was written between 2006-07 as part of a triptych on displacement co-authored with Nancy Agabian, who wrote her part in English, and Lara Aharonian, who wrote hers in French. It is a fragmentary essay, where nearly every sentence references another text. I was probably interested in putting these fragments in new relationships and constructing a certain intertextuality through allusion, quotation, and reference that would change the trajectories of the various hypotexts and lead to new links—insights. For instance, the epigraph is taken from Aurora Mardiganian's testimony, which was orally narrated in her native Armenian, interpreted by so-called "native informants" into English, and transcribed into English by American screenwriter Harvey Gates in 1917. Although Gates didn't know any Armenian, he appears as the interpreter of the Armenian narrative, which exists only in its translated form. The epigraph that appears in "Sevamenq" is not a back translation from the English text, but a new sentence that passes as a statement by Arshaluys Mardiganian (her signed name), standing as a wit-

ness to the ruptures and prostheses out of which Ravished Armenia was born.[2] *And this (in)fidelity to fact, then, is the logic in which "Blackselves" operates, threading disconnected bits of my own recollections of childhood, post-Soviet amnesia, Micheline Marcom's novel The Daydreaming Boy, a drunken conversation in a pub in Illinois with a man named Beyazit, and so on. These seemingly disparate threads evolve through a recurrent question around the notion of menq or "selves"—which might possibly refer to the authors of the triptych—Agabian, Aharonian and myself. The question of "selves" might also refer to a single construct, such as Marcom's fictional narrator Vahé Tcheubjian, who is composed of multitudes of voices, all contradicting one another. Or it could refer back to the epigraph, where the word "selves" does not occur, but which can be inferred from the self-mention marker "we": "Through the long night we waited—for what we did not know."*

But linked with the word sev or "black"—the new compound word "blackselves," and the entire piece, becomes an extended metaphor of Paul Celan's "Todesfuge." In the age of "postmemory" (Marianne Hirsch) we are not drinking black milk anymore, we have completely consumed and appropriated death, we have naturalized and neutralized grief, we no longer feel the compelling tension between "black" and "milk." The replacement of "milk" with "selves" in Armenian, written as one

[2]Mardiganian's narrative was a unique testimony of the Armenian genocide, which was adapted for the silent screen—the first of a number of motion pictures made by the Near East Relief about Armenian survivors. After losing her family and being forced into the death marches, during which she was captured and sold into the slave markets of Anatolia, and after escaping to the United States via Norway, Mardiganian was approached by Gates who proposed to make her story into film. The testimony was published in English language first as *Ravished Armenia* by Kingfield Press in New York in 1918 and as *The Auction of Souls* in London by Odhams Press in 1919. It was translated into Armenian as *Hokineru achurte* [The Auction of Souls] by Mardiros Gushagchian and published in Beirut in 1965.

word—sevamenq—creates yet another association with the word sevamaghdz (սևամաղձ), which means melancholia, literally—black bile. But this wordplay, of course, is not made explicit and not every reader will make these connections, though Celan is cited in the text. Still, if Celan is lost in the continuity of formation and deformation of meanings, the experimental text allows for another wordplay, which is more explicit and which poses a genuine challenge for the translator. The verb sevagrel or "to draft" would have had a very conventional sense in another text, but it compels a new emphasis, a new perception of drafting—literally, black-writing—when positioned against the backdrop of "blackselves." And the title of the work itself changes in the light of this verb—to draft, in other words, to be involved in the process of (re)writing the different versions of self, a process that requires resilience, elation, and exuberance. But then, herein lies the difficulty of translation—how to choose which meaning(s) to select from a web of references that construct an elaborate hypertext and how to transmit it/them to the reader, so that the reader doesn't feel completely lost or overwhelmed? After all, from its very beginnings, Armenian literature has attracted perhaps only two or three Anglo-American readers/translators (George Byron or Alice Stone Blackwell don't count) who have truly appreciated and seriously engaged with the Armenian letters.[3]

Shushan Avagyan

[3]I am infinitely grateful to Milena Abrahamyan for her radical generosity and trust in what George Steiner has called "as yet untried, unmapped alternity of statement." I would not have entrusted the translation of "Sevamenq" to anyone else, including myself.

VIOLET GRIGORYAN

"Buzz"

(poetry)

Translated by Shushan Karapetian

To the Immortal Memory of Alfred[1]

He fixed the little fold of the white table cloth, the last
glass—yes,
yes, to the right, no, it hasn't started—done, he wiped and set
it down
next to the tall shiny towers—will there be any—
leftovers?—buzz![2]
shoo!—help yourselves—just what I needed, what fine taste
you have,
straight on to the caviar, like Lusok, bread-fellow,[3]
"The woman and the buzzer: during the last supper," how
dramatic—
no, you are not late, please enter from the right—but the
"last,"—bro, c'mon,
I had just wiped it—no, I don't believe: the great one[4] would
say, even for coursework—
will I still make it?—you have to be convincing . . .
Finger foods, for small, cutsie mouthsies, white
immaculate toothsies,
the size of one bite,
Roman—ha-ha, there is no drunken elephant, but there will
be soon —

[1]Translator's Note: The reference to Alfred is to T.S. Eliot's *The Love Song of J. Alfred Prufrock*.

[2]Author's Footnote: Noise, gossip, quirks. Emotion, excitation, anything that stirs up passions, stimulation. Incomprehensible talk, curses flung through the cracks of teeth. The first single of the rock band Nirvana – *Love Buzz*. When Polonius comes to inform Hamlet that the actors have arrived, Hamlet responds, buzz, buzz, since this was no longer news. Today much news and high society gossip webpages present themselves with the word "buzz."

[3]TN: In the original Armenian, there is a play on the etymology of the word ənker (friend), which originated from əndker (eating companion).

[4]TN: The reference to the "great one" here is Stanislavski and his famous verdict, "I don't believe" to his actors'/students' performances, exhorting them to "be convincing."

arranged with a ruler, squarelets, color by color and one by
one,
Lusok cried: if you go, I'll die,
yeah they're shooting, but this is it, are these any lesser
frontlines?
stand and arrange row after row,
row after row, row after row, they come and they
g(rigi)o? [5]
softly smeared mushroom medley under clumps of cilantro,
little hams slivered to cheese,
pinchlets of asetrina[6]—what was it in Armenian? the
blessings of distance learning[7]—
shiny sparkly barbequed chicken on skewers . . .— yes?
excuse me, help yourselves, please, yes from the right—
piece-lings of dipshit—will there be any leftovers? . . .
The other is whirrlling filled glasses in a big tray
with expert acrobatics;
breaking waves[8] (saunterers' trajectory) of Nina Ricci
Christian Dior, Yves Saint Laurent
Chanel no 5, Calvin Klein . . .

---

[5]TN: In the original, there is a play on the Western Armenian kowgan ow ker/
t'an (they come and they go), with the last component t'an separated on a new line and with a question mark, standing for both the ending of the phrase "they go" and an offering of a traditional Armenian yogurt drink, t'an. This is also a reference to the repeating lines "In the room the women come and go / Talking of Michelangelo" from Eliot's *The Love Song of J. Alfred Prufrock*.

[6]TN: Commonly used Russian word for "sturgeon."

[7]TN: Distance learning is a common option in the Armenian higher education system for students who live outside of the capital or the country to gain access to university education. The quality of the education however is often considered weaker than the full-time equivalent.

[8]AF: depth, wave, internal side, womb, a mythical female evil spirit with a hideous appearance, that is an enemy of women in labor, newborns, and youth, glutton, man, and child-kidnapper.

—The cream, ha-ha, of society, how newspeak!—
will he come? how long has it been?
five or six months? acting as if I was hurt—hello, thanks a lot,
  yes, Thursday—
so he would know my worth, miss me, call after me,
instead I hear— buzz!—the good news, the little round
  bomb
ba ba boom! on me . . .
Thrift, thrift,
thrifty management of feelings,
the funeral baked-meats did coldly furnish
forth the marriage tables—no, I haven't presented
a project, well I wasn't here, you are in, right? – argh, it's
  pestering me,
shoo! Sol Partre![9]—yes, the topic is good, — to the syrup of
  my lipstick—
good luck to you, savior of women—force a smile—yes, yes,
Thursday—will he come? . . .

I should have been a pair of ragged claws . . . [10]

Here's the ambassador, with a white smile, for the sake of
  those devoted to
Toh lera unce, freehd om, and puh pah peace . . .
Puh pah pee peace,[11] yes, of course, yes, for the woman, too,

[9]TN: The character Jean-Sol Partre, a spoonerism of Jean-Paul Sartre, in Boris Vian's novel *Froth on the Daydream*.
[10]TN: Direct translation of line 73 from T.S. Eliot's *The Love Song of J. Alfred Purfrock*.
[11]TN: The intentionally deviant syllabification of these words is supposed to represent the accented and non-standard pronunciation of Armenian by some state officials to indicate their parochial and sub-standard knowledge of the language.

And for the child, Hector's scraps,[12]
but you stop becoming narrator in the process,
the only thing that's coming on to you, shoo! and only on
your lipstick: is this,
what are you to do, brains nicht, you didn't have a husband
or a proper home,
stubborn señora—

Oh, eternal feminine wail . . . [13]

Writerjournalistartistsingerpainterdesigner,
the cream . . . whoa, what's this ruckus, oh, ohh! of course,
it's he himself, his foregone majesty—who can stand it, can
you say shoo to this one? —
—the state is also pleased with this program
and participates, like so hand-in-hand—to the encircling
microphone clutter, a Hugo Boss pistil, for the Gucci, Prada,
Polo,
leaf cluster—
for our nation, defense
is our defenselessness[14]—to the tray, through tight cracks—
how newspeak!—there is no more white?—submissive,
compliant, and with a golden smile:
I'll bring it right now—and the waves—for me too!—and
more, more and more . . .

---

[12]TN: A reference to Hector, the Trojan prince in Greek mythology and his farewell to his wife Andromache. There is also a play on the rhyming words hražešt (farewell) and žešt (a Russian borrowing, meaning an old, discarded, piece of metal).

[13]TN: Marina Tsvetaeva's ironic reference to the Eternal Feminine, which is the archetypal or philosophical principle that idealizes a woman as immutable.

[14]TN: A commonly used and recognized phrase from the first president of the independent Republic of Armenia, Levon Ter-Petrossian.

I'll fuck your mother eh for our nation . . .

At night Luso—this one's Luso too—will slowly take her shirt off
her tired shoulders and before washing it: *to the camera,—*
it's the type of job where one always need to be clean, taken care of, you know? —
she'll bring it up to her nose, ah, what scents from remote worlds, a green
cape, a sailing-vessel, a star-studded hotel, chalices
full of black caviar, coralalalal, sand . . . struggle,
struggle klepto . . . [15]
—Hey, hey, look, it was this one today, there is no more wh—
ite?—he'll take his nose out, so that he can turn and look
at the television, to the small, cutsie, mouthpiece,
white, immaculate tooth demonstration—for our nation
like so, hand in hand—it was the voice of the scent of the parallel world . . .

—Here you are with red—white-lacquered delicate nails, *mmhm:* "Close up," [16]
diamond-condensed middle finger and thumb, pinky sticking out—thanks,
oops,[17] oh no—idiot, it hasn't even started; a stain on the table cloth—excuse me,
it spilled, huh, turned into a Japanese

[15]TN: A play on the correspondence of the words avaz (sand) and avazak (thief), which also forms the first root of the noun avazakapetowt'yown (kleptocracy).
[16]TN: Reference to Abbas Kiarostami's film *Close-up*.
[17]TN: English word written in Armenian transliteration.

flag . . . No worries—turn it . . . stur . . . sturgeon![18]
I remembered—turn this way—Zara, one sec, from the shoulder, and one more
excuse me-thank you—turn that way—
you know, Gaudi was wonderful, I fell in love, but it was really hot,
Paris in July, not a single museum, I've seen them all,
just sheer relaxation, oh, how I've tired from this project —
of course, you'll grow tired, ten months of the year
you're loitering about in Europe, shameless grant-eater,
constantly dilly-dallying with the consul—the middle of July?
it looks like I may have an invitation to an exhibition, perhaps we'll see each other,
umm, I don't know the location of the hotel yet—screw you! sticky gossiper—yes,
I'll tell him of course, kiss and bye bye—to Hector bye-bye,
bye-bye to Hector, bye-bye until death—how did he say it? until death
I am on your side . . . 'till death do us part, joice and rejoice,
crashing cymbals, the baked meat at the funeral repast,
with the accompanying celebrations of the welcome-baby . . .

You're good at creating melodramas,
the whole hoopla is for you; yup, there is nothing else,
what's Hector to you? or you to Hector
that you may shed a tear for him,
like some slut, measure the bile of your heart with words, wo
r r ds, yuck,
curse like a prostitute, like a house-maid,

[18]TN: The Armenian word for sturgeon.

tsk-tsk! shame on you shame on you shame on you shame on
you sh
aaaaaaaaaaaaaaaaaaaaaame—
you are hell! you are it for yourself,[19]
red-hot needles, on the lining of your dress,
red polka dots on white
yippie! and again, even sharper and sharper, even deeper . . .
Alimony for the heart—how legitimate! pah pah pah
puh pee, and no bomb or the like, eece of the granny panties
a hefty badaboom
hit your unrivaled society, alas, your unspoken tongue,
how I loved your Parthian, wimp, wuss . . .
If there were a way to become Sherlock from sissy Watson's
blah-blah
all of us wouldn't know spy Onik's address . . . [20]

I'm fine, thank you, not yet, hope you will join us[21]—
force a smile, clink your glass, pht, shoo! damned thing!
good thing I saw it early on, otherwise it would have been
an appetizer with the wine—this July? no, please[22]. . .—how
did you
say contra . . .— it's been ages—good thing he approached
me, it was the last notch of

---

[19]TN: A play on Jean-Paul Sartre's famous line "Hell is other people."

[20]TN: Reference to a popular joke about a spy named Onik, who is sent from Armenia to the US on a top-secret undercover mission. In order to establish contact with Onik they send another agent with precise instructions on how to find him. They explain that the only way to find Onik's home is by locating the pharmacy next to it. This second agent goes to the US and starts looking for Onik. He asks a random person: "Excuse me, would you tell me where to find the pharmacy?" The person responds: "No problem, go straight, turn left, ask where spy Onik's house is, everyone will show you, and right next to it is the pharmacy."

[21]TN: The entire line is in English written in Armenian transliteration.

[22]TN: "this July? no, please" is in English written in Armenian transliteration.

the childish babbling of English, — how are you, dear Gago?
— see you,[23] — oh yeah,
contract[24]—well, I've lost weight, I am on a diet,
yes, I'll eat something, uh huh, Thursday, tell Gayan—
let me smile open mouthed a bit more to this group—
probably a peach[25]—will he
come . . .?

The devil asks the Turk, the Georgian,[26]
did you see Mara's suntan? Gaudi, he-he, it was sooo hot,
ho-ho,
listen, did you see Khcho's piercing? I liked it a lot,
no way, not him, he has a lover, she's a new chick, yup, come
close so I can tell you,
but she's not a girl, you're not deaf, are you? hey girl, don't
tell anyone,
he-he, ha-ha-ha, she's a virgin, but a boy—whisper and rustle,
whisper and rustle, whisper and rustle, I am shivering slowly
cold, monotonous,
the raindom[27] washed my formless shadow, I am not you
anymore,[28]

---

[23]TN: English phrase written in Armenian transliteration.

[24]TN: English word written in Armenian transliteration.

[25]TN: Reference to line 122, "Do I dare to eat a peach?" from T.S. Eliot's *The Love Song of J. Alfred Purfrock.*

[26]TN: The first line of a popular series of jokes in the Caucasus about extraordinary circumstances that Armenians, Turks, Azerbaijanis, Russians, and Georgians are put into and their respective solutions and reactions. Typically these involve an encounter with the devil, God, a dinosaur or some powerful force, which sets up certain conditions, often reflecting the geopolitical environment of the time. In the Armenian context, the Armenian typically comes up with the most witty, clever, and/or humorous solution.

[27]TN: A play on the similar sounds in the words anjrew (rain) and janjrowytʻ (boredom) from poet Vahan Teryan.

[28]TN: The preceding three lines contain references to some well-recognized lines and themes (whisper and rustle, shivering slowly, cold, monotonous, formless shadow, I am not you anymore) by Ar-

I am an owl, squeak-squeak!
did you eat my coconut?[29] how was the taste of my . . . [30] Oh,
thanks, thanks,
where did I leave my lighter?—a rhetorical question
for the supposedly fiery Prometheus . . .

—We've gathered nicely, we can start the revolutio . . .
—Hey man, for once, allow us—when did his majesty
approach?—to breathe
calmly, your revo, I'll be damned! That
lution will not run away to the forest,
leave it for tomorrow—amicable laughter, Turk and Georgian,
Zara and Mara, Gago and Khcho, devil and Gaudi, revolt
and bolt, whisper and rustle,
ow, my stomach, yes, need to eat,
perhaps a peach, Alfie? perhaps, per
haps, the wine numbed me and the elitescented
waves, ah, I wonder, who pops your
pimples? my revolutionized—well, the microphone,
will I still make it? they are just prepping it—
and that one with the big yellow head,
that would always sprout under your right shoulder blade—
hey, did you notice
the blonde midget? the yellow head,
barely under the arm—oops, am I already speaking out loud

menian poet Vahan Teryan.

[29]TN: Reference to the popular children's poem and cartoon, "Powy powy mknik" (Squeak, squeak, little mouse) by Derenik Demirchyan about a little mouse who lives under a coconut tree. One day a coconut falls down and the mouse struggles to get inside through a crack. After much difficulty, the mouse gets in and gluttonously drinks all of the coconut liquid, after which he struggles to come out.

[30]TN: Reference to the following 1916 quatrain by Hovhannes Toumanyan: In my dream an ewe/ Came up to me with a question,/"May God protect your son,/ How was the taste of my child?"

to myself?—but how she's landed
the sugar daddy—velvet and fur, violin, piano—
now do you know why they're fucking?[31]—
don't exaggerate—did I say it out loud again?—ten fingers
  and a tongue,
she does a good job of paying him back with grateful
fake orgasms, aah aah aah—
I'll buy it, I'll buy it[32]—on his favorite piece of beautiful
  furniture—
my bed, do you remember how it snap! and I still haven't
  fixed it,
the Bible, a dictionary, of the old East, the new West,
poetry, and so on, well
according to its thickness . . . Will the velvet lady
pop pimples?

A woman's bed, full of sorrow . . . [33]

Perhaps a peach, perhaps, perhaps, per
haps, will you eat a peach for life? or co
still conut? still swell, still fart
in front of the velvet lady? drums with your behind . . .

Ah, the mournful sobbing of my violin . . . [34]

---

[31]TN: Russian word in Armenian transliteration.

[32]TN: Reference to a line from the movie *Pepo* by one of the main characters, the aging nouveau riche Zimzimov, who constantly buys new things to impress his new, young wife.

[33]TN: Reference to the play *Medea* by Euripides.

[34]TN: Reference to Armenian poet Vahan Teryan.

Oh, who now massages your feet?
who wipes your forehead with lotion?
holds your face with two palms
pressing your lids with both thumbs—
take off your glasses, do you see
up close? tell me,
and what do you see?—
important things? with your eye?[35] no way,
oh, if you would play
kitty-kitty—
in the Luxembourg gardens . . .
But are there Luxembourg gardens in the world?
where does the red flag hit the thorny scarlet rose
beyond words?
where is the bee—that is not seen, but heard—speaking
  buzz-ish
in his ear?
and does the wind retain the whizzing of the z during
  translation?
or does it tatter one by one and each and every z
takes a letter to the fields far from the dandelions . . .
But are there dandelions? are the fields
on the other side of the hill there? is the sun there? is there a
  star
and moon? does the water plummet from the river to the
  ravine?
but is the ravine there
beyond words?
If there is sun, then why do the mornings rise in black

[35]TN: Reference to *The Little Prince* by Antoine de Saint-Exupéry.

darkness?
if there is water, why am I thirsty?
if the bee exists, why did the scarlet-red rose wither in my
hand?
if there is the ravine, who is that jumping off
that is not the self? but . . . heartless girl . . . [36]

No, don't lie to me, there is no one, they are not here,
I've seen them in a parallel place, in another world,
here there are words that confirm them,
but now they are already bearing false witness,
but now they are already their graves,
but now they already smell like death,
but now already . . .

How far away is the parallel world from the heart of your
heart? . . .

One, two,[37] parallel, yes, it sounds good, three prizes:
1. best
2. best
annnd, the bes . . .
annnd, the bes . . .
my very first, my Turk, my Georgian, my devil, my Gaudi—
waves of emotion and the stink of sweat
from the corners and cracks of ChanelGucciBoss . . .
—I wasn't doing my work for the medal or the prize—

---

[36]TN: Reference to the homonymous poem and opera *Anush*, in which the heroine commits suicide by throwing herself off a cliff.
[37]TN: Both words are in English in Armenian transliteration.

the champagne was mine, that's for Nvard, she was just here,
that green-turquoise over there—
yeah, what did I want to say, may the worthy be appreciated.
—Well, of course, ok, I am going to go eat something, probably
a peach, I am on a diet, say hello to Nvush
if I don't see her, and breaking the waves,
lacerating, la-cerrrrr-attt-ing . . .

I broke the waves so you, so I, so
that you could rise up
here today, shit on me—what a causeandeffect
conclusion—
kick me in my stupid ass, throw me on the ground and wipe your feet on me,
just like this line, row after row, like an army of long-legged glasses
men were lined up in front of me, oh, frailty, thy name . . . what?—
ah these women, love over and over love over and over love . . .

But of course, I wasn't doing my project for a medal or a prize,
the important part is to participate, we are all for the same important goal—listen, did you see?
this harlot's ex-fucker has already come with his wife,
she probably still hasn't seen them, when I said: it wasn't for the prize, she smirked,
now go and laugh over there, did you see how she had lost

weight? Laurel-Hardy,
probably from active masturbation, he-he, a cigarette
in her expert fingers, always a cigarette, yuck, fake,
cuckoo loony old woman, she's completely lost it,
she's already talking to her self, uh huh, enough already, one-two,
one-two, we said it sounds good already, like a fly she meddles in everything, nutty
fucker, say hel-loo to Nuh-vush, someone should ask, does Nvush
even give a shit about you, can I tell you something for real: would you believe it
if I said I don't even care, whoever it'll be, as long as it's not Nvard, with her father's position
everywhere . . .

I trampled on my father's crown, the golden fleece your prize,
I tore my brother to pieces, threw him in the sea,
I abandoned my home, my own shore, I abandoned my homeland in the water,
My pair of children, I . . . [38]
—You don't have a child to pop the pimple?—
you are hell, you for yourself, when there is someone else sitting
inside of you—
o virgin kiss-ass daughter of Babylon, blessed is the one,
who will repay you your recompense,
who will treat you the way,

[38]TN: These four lines are reference to Euripidies' *Medea*.

that you have treated others,
blessed is the one, who will take your child from you,
and smash him on the rocks,
Oh, dear Kikos, oh, dear Kikos . . . [39]

Through the waves through the waves through the waves,
hey, careful, little one, where are you running? where did
  you come from? what's your name?
where is your brother?
my mom has your, she has your smell too,
what about this, does she have some of this?—
a prize for the protection of oppressed women—
oh my prize, my red medal,
on someone else's chest,
a prize for finding women,
for putting a tongue in their mouth,
and with that same tongue, for mouthing off—mhm, you
  were one of the judges, right?
you know, in the villages it's only darkness,[40]
just like the middle ages,
they beat women, can you believe it? those same wretched
  ones,
who toil in the fields all day, in dung and, you know?[41] this
  bullshit,[42]
and in the kitchen, I mean everywhere[43]—

---

[39]TN: Reference to a tale by Armenian writer Hovhannes Toumanyan, entitled "The Death of Kikos," about a young woman who envisions getting married, having a child, and that child climbing a tree and falling to his death. The entire family then mourns the death of the child.
[40]TN: Russian word in Armenian transliteration.
[41]TN: English phrase in Armenian transliteration.
[42]TN: English phrase in Armenian transliteration.
[43]TN: English phrase in Armenian transliteration.

sorry,[44] hey Nvard? they were looking for you—the men get drunk, go
home and beat those miserable ones, to whom they have not given even
one drop of love, no warmth and no care, what language is that in? with what do they
eat with?—sexual object—that's it, nothing else,[45]
excuse me, tell me, why are you in a flutter, girl? they still haven't announced the prize . . . whaaat,
yes, I saw, I saw,
and that's the object, he-he, sexual, she'll see right now, you'll see how her head
has remained bowed, she can't take care of her own issues, she is solving other
women's problems . . .

Hey, idiot women, hey, Dridorian[46]
ten girlies, down there,[47] for whom have you
painted yourself scarlet red? or should I send you the good news in the mail? for the lot of you
snoring in the donkey's ear,[48] ill—
informed sluts, are you still waiting for that majestic facade, on which
you've inflated your egos so? . . . Now watch how I am
shredding you into pieces,
shredding and discarding,

[44]TN: English word in Armenian transliteration.

[45]TN: English phrase in Armenian transliteration.

[46]TN: Reference to Violet Grigoryan's last name being printed incorrectly as Dridoryan.

[47]TN: Reference to Alice looking down at her feet in *Alice in Wonderland*.

[48]TN: Play on the Armenian proverb/saying êši akan⊠owm k⊠nac (asleep in the donkey's ear) indicating someone who remains unaware of something important.

and needle by needle, under the nailzz, sprrrraying rrrred
on rrrred, on the blood, sprrrrinkling a good dosse of salt,
garrrrlic, and pepperrr,
how I am brrringing you to yourrr
kneezzz, on a sharrrp shingle, so faccce to faccce
arrrm in arrrm, waillll like that, I am going to wrrrring
poizzon
from your grrrroanz and whisperzz—
—Mr. President, here is the white—
and a pearl, for thy heal(th) . . . oh my,
hey girl, oh my, it/he/she[49] fell . . .
Perhaps the rope was too thin, girl, perhaps, per
haps—
well it's ok, nothing was left in it/him/her,[50]
but for the new little one, that is going to be born, perhaps it
would be enough—
yes, it's a good little one, minus the footnotes, over 300 . . .
No! don't hit it with the trophy, girl, yuck, how you smashed
it . . .
Oh, eternal feminine buzzing (3 threes) . . .

cut[51]

---

[49]TN: The grammatical flexibility of Armenian allows the reference here to be intentionally ambiguous. Since Armenian is a null-subject language, an explicit subject is not required in the original. Moreover, Armenian has one genderless third person singular personal pronoun, which can stand for he/she/it.

[50]TN: Same as note 49.

[51]TN: Originally in English.

Violet Grigoryan's brilliance lies in her masterful interlacing of the repertoire of various social and dialectal registers of Armenian along with a fluid multilingualism that is taken for granted by a group so accustomed to having multiple languages—and their accompanying sociolinguistic resources—readily available in any setting. The torturous yet gratifying process of attempting to translate these intra- and interlingual leaps has challenged and stretched the boundaries of my own linguistic reserves.

On a deeper level, however, the entire poem confronts the notion of translation, as, at its core, it is an attempt to decode the raw, fleeting, and chaotic thoughts of various characters battling their double consciousness, while Grigoryan simultaneously challenges her own awareness of the limitations of the poetic medium. Constantly testing the reader's tolerance for ambiguity, she surreptitiously shifts narrator, linguistic media, and modes of speech. Grigoryan immerses us in and draws us out of her characters' inner thoughts and external utterings, flavored by the commentary of various social types attending a high society event, who look on in amused contempt and pity. In capturing the transition between the uncontrollable firing of thoughts to their ensuing verbal expression, all kinds of identities are put to the test: linguistic, gender, social, national, and political. Grigoryan presents a woman wronged by an unrequited love as the central heroine, a character obsessed with revenge and plagued with an inability to decipher if her thoughts are indeed her own or those imposed on her by society. The lines that read, "You are hell, you for yourself, when there is someone else sitting / inside of you," capture the angst of the woman's double consciousness. But just as the woman is victim to social and gender norms set by man and society, so language is victim to the forces of the uncontrolled, frenzied, and tumultuous stream of consciousness of the main characters. Although Grigoryan challenges the conventions of the poetic medium in a multitude of ways in order to realize this transition from chaotic thought to physical utterance, she is still paralyzed by her consciousness of the tradition. Even in her deliberate deviance from linguistic conventions—ranging from lexical, semantic, phonological, to the usage of dialect and a variety of registers and languages—she is still left with an uneasy search for a parallel universe beyond words. As she articulates in the poem, the current world has words that confirm certain phenomena, "But now they are already bearing false witness, / but now they are already their graves."

Shushan Karapetian

EDUARD HAKHVERDIAN

"Prodigal Son"

(poetry)

Translated by Lilit Keshishyan

I

Now, when
The city's crooked and blemished face
Is coated in white anguish,
And in each fold of the brain
Exists a cruel mania of lethal saws.

Now, when
The temple's domes
Are fused with white mist,
And the unsuspended crosses
Blessing nothing
are bolted, motionless, in the air.

Now, when
In the gardens of paradise
The trees of our childhood dreams
Topple mercilessly,
And the dismal chimneys of painful moans
Quickly burn
The asteroids of our fragile souls
Reducing them to smoke and soot.

Now, when
The gray wolf's bloody paws
Insatiably scratch
The roofless expanse of
A glorious history,
And the rising tree's branchless morality

Slowly rots
Waiting for no victims . . .

Now, when
The white anguish
Snows from the soul's sky
Onto the dark streets of noxious days,
And phantom hands of terror
Paint black crosses on houses,
And the houses are encased in iron bars,
And the trees are encased in iron bars,
And slowly
With a cold, arachnoid silent patience,
With the insatiable mania for steel and metal,
Our souls become barricaded
And the weapon,
denying its bankrupt mission,
in the heights of vulgarity
stabs
the bloodless belly of a dying justice.

Now, when
In lethal darkness of the houses
The crippled, crazy,
gray masks
unflinchingly watching
through the shattered mirror,
Are tortured.

Now, when
The moan,
The cry,
The wail
having become an iceberg
clogged
in the strained vocal chords
Oh, don't ask, don't ask
How
Anchored like a sphynx
I became
PRODIGAL SON

II

The white roofs,
The white trees,
The white streets
Don't witness winter.
This is an omen of torn masks,
This is an omen of a kind of payment,
This is the omen of a sweet joy,
This is the omen of self-discovery.
The torment of the white anguish
From the soul's abyss,
Like the boulder of Sisyphus,
Rolls infinitely
From Spring to Winter,
From Winter to Spring,
And our portion of life's joy,

Is the delight of the color of the mountain's rock,
The unnamed flower's luminous charm,
The flapping of the unknown bird's wings
Planting grief in the garden of memories,
Is the charm of the word,
In glide of speech,
The liberation of the paint,
The delight of the color on the canvas,
And our portion of life's joy
Is seeking truce with the bombs,
Is the panic
Of having lost the thread of our salvation
In the labyrinth of uncertainty.
In grandiosely making sense of
Our uncertain, meaningless days
In the noisy taverns
In the madness of the grapes
In the message of silence
It is the
Punctual
Provision of survival coupons
Every hour,
Every day,
Every year,
Every season
It is in plugging with our torn bodies
The open barrel
of Pandora's
disasters,

and malice.
It is in the pleasure of coffee
In a dark corner
With the pipe of patience.
It is in illuminating, with the brightness of love,
heaven and hell,
Chaos, purgatory,
The Beginning and the End,
In becoming the wick in love's lamp,
The blending of all matter
With the matter of love,
Because the portion of life's joy
Is the joy of Sisyphus,
And the boulder of our suffering
Is cast in the valley,
And the boulder of our destiny,
Is cast in the valley,
And the boulder of our daily life,
Is cast in the valley
And our portion of life's joy
Is our slow and steady
Approach to suffering,
Our luminous perception
Of our life and destiny,
Our luminous,
Luminous,
Neglect
Of our life and destiny.

III

Oh, winds, vulgar and blind . . .

My father came in, his head shaved, he didn't curse, he didn't show anger

and didn't request compensation for innocence. The black saliva of blind anguish strewn on the cell wall, he quietly gathered the gold chain of silence and silently departed, his heart bursting with yearning and a blood-choked cry.

Oh, winds, vulgar and blind . . .

His eye on my eye, his lips on my lips, his heart on my heart, he stood, perplexed and dumbstruck. He didn't complain, didn't scold, and having left the sack of laughter at customs, he sprinkled his laughter's last crumbs as dots of life and departed. And he didn't hear the silent explosion of my wounded heart, and didn't see, the heavy procession of trains over me, always without me on board.

Oh, winds, vulgar and blind . . .

How many thousands of flowers and grass, how many thousands of cuttings and trees, where did your hellish laughter shatter, break, blow away, from these dark and heavenly shores. Oh, winds, vulgar and blind . . .

What kind of harvest is this on Spring's doorstep? What gale of mourning is rushing up, destroying the apricot tree of our awakening?

Oh, winds, vulgar and blind . . .

IV

Now, when everyone is prepared for escape
Now, when everyone walks around with their suitcases,
Now that the centuries old staff of exile, with a kind of
 wizardry has turned
into a magical wand,
I,
As winter's only fuel,
And the only ointment for nerves
strained like a bow,
tear apart Anahid's portrait, far from aesthetics,
tear apart the unsent love letters
for Anahid, far from aesthetics,
And many other canvases, far from aesthetics,
And many other books, far from aesthetics,
And many other papers, far from aesthetics,
And next to the fireplace, blushing with shame,
I sing the saddest song of winter
about warmth.

Everything is heading towards vanity,
Everything is heading towards vanity.

Countless steps descend from the sky
And the tanks with the trail of blood tulips
Head toward the east,
And the soldiers,
Shivering like leaves in the wind,
With backpacks of death

Head toward the east.
And the doctors,
Weighed down by Hippocrates' heavy hat,
Head toward the east.
And painters,
And poets,
And scientists,
And those who are volunteers,
And those who haven't had the chance to flee,
With the trail of blood tulips
Head towards the east,
And the mania to kill,
The fever to kill,
With the will of the high ranking lords
Becomes the only target.

V

I don't search for anything in the trash pile . . .

I was flying in my dream while singing all the moments of my life, I have torn the cocoon of hopelessness to flying in the light of faith. Who, again, has cast a net on the blue? Who has nailed my wings to the cliff?

I don't search for anything in the trash pile . . .

I have, without pain, left my blooming flowerbeds so that I can make the flower growing in the rock's crevice, the only thing to lean on . . .

I don't search for anything in the trash pile, but here, on my breast, the yellow flower, opened in the heart of the trash heap, glitters like a pin.

I don't search for anything in the trash pile . . .

VI

Again, I bow to your grass
To your every flower and stone,
And "not-being" is never an issue,
And the answer is as simple
And as sharp
As the path of the unswerving bullet
From barrel to temple.

Like fish caught in your net
We are still fluttering, still flapping
Don't can us like sardines
In coffins
For the sake of shutting the jaw of the multi-mouthed earth.

Yet another winter,
Yet another spring,
Yet another summer—
And the ubiquitous falling of leaves
And the caravan of failed days
Like a dagger
Cutting our existence to pieces
Incessantly revolves
Around circle of the four seasons.

Oh, don't take me,
Don't take me
To the red-grassed pastures
I don't want to see the massacre of the tulips . . .
And "not-being" is never an issue,
And the answer is as simple
And as sharp
As the path of the unswerving bullet
From barrel to temple . . .

Eduard Hakhverdyan is a poet, translator, and painter living in Armenia. His poem "Prodigal Son" provides a literary reflection on the harsh circumstances that plagued Armenia after its independence from the Soviet Union in 1991. Often referred to as the "dark years," the period between 1992 and 1995 is marked by the literal and symbolic darkness faced by Armenia due to fuel and food shortages caused by energy blockades, war, and a failing infrastructure. As translator, I was tasked to communicate the visceral quality of Hakhverdyan's words and tone into English and capture the concurrent hopelessness and resiliency of its speaker. Similar to Hakhverdyan's other works, "Prodigal Son" uses the personal, the literal, and the specific to effectively communicate a collective, and indeed universal, account of desperation and survival.

Lilit Keshishyan

ANNA DAVTYAN

"In the Name of Buttons"

(poetry)

Translated by the Author

third master

The president leans over, and the four buttons on his sleeve
inscribe their stamp
while he draws traces in some history.
Four wheels—longwise,
faceless like the nature—
tree, tree, tree, tree,
witness like the nature
on a dark sidewalk.
Four buttons
of a small country, of a big country,
of a country of small towns
bending—over inks and paper, over crowds, and disasters,
under the sun, over the bogs
like storks. Eight eyes upon four roots—
sewn with a thread. A thread of doubts.

second master

Fly fast, run rapid, swim swift,
escape easy, prey-beast!
The tribe chief sings to the prey—
My hunter will catch you with bare hands,
choose your goddess, prey-beast!
The naked hunter plays the water, the earth, the leaves, the
moon,
in the sun,
the small straw bunch is his clothing with

bone buttons—
the sign of his vigor,
sewn with beast tissues,
Run fast, prey-beast!
He's already finished his playing
sewn to the forests—with steady threads.

first master

She circles around, and her circles include what concerns the man and herself.
Having the peel of obedience, weakness and beauty
she circles pots of the sound mind, taking from one side of the earth
and giving to the other.
She rearranges the hunting site with a thousand hands—
originally knows the order of things correctly,
possesses power over all concerns,
over the man,
that ceaselessly provides weapons to be cleaned,
and over the buttons that are firmness and beauty.
She is on the earth by the knee, and the earth of all times is all in her hands.
She–Ursula.

I have translated the following poem word for word—a process that does not deal in equivalencies in English that would translate the same in Armenian. Rather, going beyond transference to grasping the internal meaning, interpreting a word already deconstructed in order to understand, not after understanding. What has the word for word translation to offer? It helps to bring into the target language the foreign glow of a text, and beyond that, what the source language already has to offer—what Walter Benjamin calls "pure language." Languages operate as spies in the depository of pure language, complementing each other's knowledge through texts. If I were a language my dream would not be clinging to what is already known, but in guessing more. This text with its Armenian glow is there for that.

Anna Davtyan

MAROUSH YERAMIAN

"Aleppo, Aleppo"

"Without Exit"

(poetry)

Translated by Michael Pifer

Aleppo, Aleppo

The soil wasn't mine

but it became mine
when my grandfathers were buried there.
They had come
with the dream of the USA
from Dikranagerd
to here

where the sky had sprinkled a glaucous dream
in their dreamless,
anguished souls

where the crimson soil had given birth
to wheat, to bread
to an unrealized faith in sweet life.

The soil wasn't mine

but it became mine

when my *hani* was born here
my grandmother
who went by *Khanum*[1]

(she was renamed
Zvart Kasbarian)

[1]A woman of rank in Iran or Turkey (the modern Turkish equivalent is *hanım*).

and at her wedding
with a jaundiced smile and arms raised
she danced '*lemune al-lemune*' fervently.

The language wasn't mine
but the echo reached my ear
from distant
Ani, from king Gagik,[2]

and from our history's flowing plait:
securely woven by many hands,
undone by the same
nomadic
races.

But the pain was ours, mine from the beginning:
the pain of tortured earth and spilt blood was mine
(for both were equal, the same)

upon this soil
blue in blood
and in this tongue

I was this place
            and this place was mine, just as the forest
or the heavens belong to the hind.

But the fire came down;

---

[2]The medieval city of Ani, located today in eastern Turkey, was the capital of the Bagratid Kingdom of Armenia.

heaven renounced her children
who remained landless, skyless,

and who were lost
in a place between
reality and the evening news.

The place disowned us
along with the sky;
we, who exalted it upon our shoulders
and cared for it by the shade of our eyelashes.

The swallows were late for their rendezvous
(in the afternoon of every spring
at 4 o'clock)
with children released from school
and the cascading blessing
of evening.

Heaven was pierced with holes

and the swallows don't understand—
why there were no boys of the "wooden square"
awaiting them?

Or why were their no sellers of *zeit* and *zaatar*?[3]
There was only a petrifying, pregnant silence
—silence, as if, a female—

[3]*Zeit* is the Arabic word for olive oil; *zaatar*, or thyme, is often prepared as a common seasoning mixed with sesame seeds, sumac, and salt.

ready, at any moment, to birth terror.

Under the pierced sky
there was a pierced map
where we had stopped,
had found a foothold in this place.

Over us,
the blessings of swallows

from whom we learned to sing
during our nights around the citadel
sweetened by the fragrance of hookahs.

In those days,
time was our friend:
the deep blue of night
would smoke with us
and would sing duets, ballads of the old knights
whose names were engraved
on the gates
of the citadel:

"I neither forget
nor remember the future . . ."
(the latter, arm-in-arm with time,
slipped out of our city,
leaving behind dust,
oblivion)

now, a place, in a pit of the earth,
in the presence of forgotten monasteries, we draw breath
the tenderness of turtledoves warbling
over our shoulders.

Without Exit

I kneaded the earth
and my hands bled.
the brooks bled
and the verdure burned
but still I kneaded,
opening casks of royal,
ancient oil,
sifting for salt
in a lake of tears.

Look, there
under August's sun
dreams are desiccated,
furrow by furrow;
rats gnaw on the buds.

The mysterious
subterranean tunnels of old
have consigned the echoing cry of *ya-leyl*
— *oh night!* — to clay jugs;
the toothless mouths of old women
have frozen
in a curse toward heaven.
        Corpses fester there.
The gurgling of basins on the *iwan*
has fallen silent in dread.
There's no soul left
who might question the ruins.

Our surroundings, strained from the beginning
grow tighter,
constricting like a noose:
it's impossible to draw even a half-a-breath.

And we tear apart
the Arabian courtyards of our inner-worlds:
the red soil spills forth from the pots,
abandoned plants wither.
So we rip down garlands,
fine ornamentation
looking for the snake
who, until now, has been the *uğur*,
the good luck of home.
Was he just a fairy-tale
told after dark?

We are always awake, even now.
But—
why does the nightmare continue on?
The church bell-tower is gone
there's no ringing
to rouse us from this longing.

Why did we cast down the staff?
it was necessary to go far:
to seek immortality in the corners of disappearance.

We, the vagrant,
we search, wandering, for our secrets—

why did we cast down the staff?
we threw off our shoes
and surrendered to oblivion
the road to heaven

the road
that always winds through hell.

the pigeons still live together:
their numbers grow strong.

"The worst place in the world?" asks the headline of an article from The Guardian on March 12, 2015. "Aleppo in ruins after four years of civil war." Certainly, these two poems by Maroush Yeramian draw from a poetics of destruction in which the principal characters — displaced persons, abandoned buildings, and warbling turtledoves — bring to life a cityscape that oscillates between the highly intimate and the jarringly alien.

Yeramian, who was born and lived much of her life in Aleppo, has observed the decimation of her country firsthand. However, it would be a mistake to assume these translations reductively "witness" the tragedy of the Syrian civil war to an international audience. As Yeramian asserts, the inhabitants of her poems are lost "in a place between / reality and the evening news." By extension, these poems do something that neither "reality" nor the "evening news" can offer. To read them only for information, as though perusing a newspaper, would risk missing something essential about the representational mode that Yeramian employs.

Where is this "place between," the place where poetry offers an alternative to the twin pitfalls of reporting and witnessing? To a limited extent, it is located in Yeramian's language, as these poems weave Arabic and Turkish words into a Western Armenian context. This intersection of lexicons would be familiar to any Armenian living in the Middle East; it reflects not only the hybridity of a diasporic experience, but also a way of living and being in Aleppo as an Armenian. Rather than erase this lexicon, my translations do not replace Arabic and Turkish words with their English equivalents. That said, the intimacy of Yeramian's lexicon is also reversed here: to an English reader, words like uğur and ya-leyl might now evoke a foreign quality.

We can find a similar reversal in the original language as well. These poems explore the literal translation of Aleppo's cityscape into something unrecognizable: an intimacy inverted. It's this uncanny interplay between familiar and foreign, interior and exterior, intimate and other that constitutes Yeramian's poetics in Armenian. Therefore, I have sought to generate an analogous interplay here, even though our frames of reference must necessarily change.

Michael Pifer

IKNA SARIASLAN

“West Side Story”

“Laborer of Love”

“LO”

(poetry)

Translated by Alec Ekmekji

West Side Story

the ticket queues were extended
along Yesilçam Street
many times—oh so many times
we went to see West Side Story
at the Emek cinema
Intoxicated by Lenny's tunes
we floated on his love songs

in the queues
on Yesilçam Street
we'd remember our languished loves
and we'd pave it with the clay
of the loves that were to come

West Side Story was purple rain

Laborer of Love

I loved without punctuation
I loved without comma

New line they said—no I said
Line break they said quotes they said—no I said

Without pausing
Without striking I loved

My love inexhaustible ink
My love infinite line
My love endless letter

So I intoxicated
Didn't sign the letter

I loved without hesitation
I loved without comma

Could love have been eternity?
Or eternity love?—I did not learn.

LO

On the same hour Saturday
beneath the clock at the pier
I wait for you Lo
We walk hand in hand toward Muhurdar
we sit—we watch the sunset
intoxicated—intoxicated Lo
At that hour
the sun is a bleeding plum above the mosques
tea has the color of your lips
the flavor of your kiss Lo
Then we roam the streets of Moda
where the trees carved with your name
greet us like an honor guard
which we inspect one by one
And if you so desire we hire a small boat
with you—for you I conjugate the verb to love
as the boat dances on the waves yes beautiful!

And when the moon wanders on the celestial vault
we walk toward Kalamesh Lo
Look at the pier of Kalamesh
how dark it is
how desolate

And if you wish we drift toward Fenerbahçe
we catch sight of the islands
the ships sailing back and forth
the lights of the ships

the hopes of the stars
and the ardor of our souls
On the benches of Fenerbahçe
I carve hearts torn by arrows
I kiss the stones of all the roads you've traveled
I kiss them all—I kiss them Lo
It is enough that you come Lo
Saturday at the same hour
Beneath the clock of the pier at Kadiköy
It will suffice
It will suffice my goddess

O Lo—O Lola—Laura

Several years ago, I began to translate poetry from Armenian to English and quickly discovered that it enhanced my understanding of the poems. This was, of course, due to the multiple and repetitive readings of the poems within a short amount of time—often aloud, the dissection of sentences and phrases, and the sometimes futile attempts of rearranging words to remain true to both the new language and the original.

In translating poetry, my objective and measure of success becomes to say nothing more and nothing less than the original, with minimal deviation from the rhythms and textures—yes, that elusive texture!—of the original, and most importantly without hinting that this is a translation. In these translations of Ikna Sariaslan's three poems, I started by reading as much of his poetry as I could find on the Internet. I read many of them several times, and often out loud so I could hear the rhythms. I had not been familiar with his work when I accepted to translate his poetry.

The poem "Laborer of Love" was the most interesting and challenging to navigate because of the abundantly delicate interactions between phrases and meanings.

This poem comprises seven short stanzas, each with either two or three lines. The fourth stanza, positioned at the center of the poem, is remarkable in that it deviates from the general structure of the other stanzas in interesting ways. Its three lines show significant similarities and symmetries: each line contains three words, the first words of its lines are the same, the second words of its lines are adjectives with the prefix un-, and the last words are nouns that refer to act of writing. Furthermore, the stanza contains no verbs—only nouns and adjectives while all other stanzas are comprised of complete sentences. Together, they produce a rhythm that is abrupt and a texture that is jagged. With this brusqueness the stanza suddenly stands and declares its impatience, but is quickly overruled by the stanzas that follow and restore the original rhythm and texture to the poem.

So how does one capture this structural turmoil in a translation?

I started with:

My love line without beginning
My love abundant ink
My love letter without end

But this translation did not capture the effect of the original. After a few days, multiple re-readings out loud, and several iterations, it morphed into:

My love infinite line
My love inexhaustible ink
My love unending letter

This brought me closer to the poem's vision, yet I felt the translation had a few issues: first, "inexhaustible" had too many syllables; second, "unending" seemed as if a verb was trying to sneak in; and third, the word "line" seemed ambiguous. In Armenian, the word for a line of verse is specifically referred to as "dogh," which is what appears in the original. English does not offer such a word. I changed the order of the lines in order to limit the ambiguity of the word "line," and I replaced the word "unending" with "endless." Thus, the stanza became:

My love inexhaustible ink
My love infinite line
My love endless letter

As a last effort, I wanted to replace "inexhaustible" with "luxuriant" because I sought to use a shorter word for the adjectives, as the poet had done. But that word seemed to convey more than the Armenian, and my instinct told me not to do it; so I relented.

Translating this poem, and particularly conveying this turmoil in another language, was engaging. This sort of expression of structural chaos also appears in music. As I navigated through these obstacles I could not help but hear the repeated bursts of unexpected chords in the second movement of Beethoven's Third Symphony. In this respect, the poem and the symphony seemed to mirror each other across the boundary of two centuries.

Alec Ekmekji

ARAM PACHYAN

"Remembering the Reader"

(fiction)

Translated by Nairi Hakhverdi

I walk up to the window at the break of dawn and look for birds. The birds fall from the roof of a tall building and suddenly soar back up, defying the relentlessness of motion, and scatter like ash. They replace my morning readings. I have many unfinished novels: on my desk, in libraries, in my sister's room, in my car. Last week, I was getting myself in the mood to reread Goncharov's *Oblomov* or any one of Philip Roth's works. I pick up *Oblomov* and start off quite well. Soon I stop, take a leafy bookmark out of a drawer, and lay it flat between pages forty-three and forty-four. That's it. I won't continue, I know it. I only read the first three paragraphs of one of Philip Roth's novels and put it down. I've been finding myself in front of unfinished stories a lot lately. I stop and for a few minutes I look indecisively at the letters of the name of the writer or the work. It seems to me that when I look indecisively, I look sadly. The bookmark sticking out of the book resembles the tongue of a lifeless cat. I will never resume the book from where I left off and I will never return to the beginning. The book turns to self-defense. Approaching it is death. The existence of my unfinished books reminds me of my own fragmentation. How well I now understand the hero of one of my favorite childhood cartoons, Pinocchio, and his desire to turn from wood into flesh and blood, or Achilles and Jesus who probably suffered the most from malnutrition!

I'm often beginning to feel like a bitten apple on top of a cupboard that has long been forgotten and that is neither thrown away, nor eaten up. Now I can say that I'm one of those left unfinished. I'm the one who abandons a road halfway. I abandon the road, but I don't have another. I've gone from being a reader to a page-turner. I pick up a book, I open to a random page, and read the gifted or weak lines: words that resemble undulating grass and words that have the coldness of copper wires sticking out of slabs of concrete. What I find is only a piece of the bigger problem. It's a pity no one will get offended. The writers whose novels are always with me are long gone and they can't see how I corrupt their wholeness one after another, how I finish dozens of years and hours in an instant. They are powerless in protecting the trace of the life they left behind.

I'm reading "Combray," the first chapter of the first volume of Marcel Proust's serial novel. During his insomnia, little Marcel's feelings and thoughts extend like the day of a bedridden patient who suddenly dies in his sleep, unaware of the day's continuation. In his book *Portraits-Souvenirs*, Cocteau recalls an event related to Proust. When they visit the writer, he suddenly breaks off the conversation and the reading, leaves the room, and doesn't return for a long time. Cocteau goes after him and finds Proust in the bathroom gorging down noodles. Marcel was bringing his work to an end.

Days go by.

I live, remembering myself.

Every night my father read passages from his favorite authors and returned to one of them as if he had finished it. We would take breaks around the table set for tea, enjoying cornelian cherry jam and walnut cake. My father's smile would glide from the brim of his cup to my face, and I would smile back at him in the same way and turn the seed of the cornelian cherry faster in my mouth. He would suddenly get up and run to his room, return with a book and reread his favorite passage. He has never read an entire work out loud. For him, the passage in the book that bestowed delight and amazement never ended, but the book did.. By clinging onto the passage, he made every effort to save that brief moment of happiness, and by returning to it he tried to repeat that same happiness. I don't know, maybe my father is the one I got my incompleteness from. I, too, constantly return to my favorite passages in books, vanishing in the full images of life. I probably want to repeat myself in my father's happiness and press myself against it, turning reality into a fairy tale. I'm neither in books nor in life. There is no "in-between" for me. Right now there are only shrieks and death throes. A novel that begins with a sentence and a novel that ends with a sentence. And in the space that stretches between the sentences everything is the same, unchanging. And since the unknown is the beginning and the end, I pick up one of my favorite books without any responsibility or shame, and read the first and last sentence out loud:

"It was in those days when I wandered about hungry in Kristiana, that strange city which no one leaves before it has set its mark upon him . . ."[1]

"Once out in the fjord I straightened up, wet with fever and fatigue, looked in towards the shore and said goodbye for now to the city, to Kristiania, where the windows shone so brightly in every home."[2]

---

[1]From Knut Hamsun, *Hunger*, translated by Sverre Lyngstad, Canongate Books, Digital Edition, 2008.

[2]*Ibid.*

It's evening. I'm drinking mulled wine at café Achajur, sip by sip moving into the red thickness. The cloves at the bottom of the glass look like sleeping fish. I don't know if I'll get to them. I don't excuse myself, without reason, and continue drinking my wine. Maybe I'll start reading a new novel tomorrow or maybe this very night I'll take the thickest book from my library and read until dawn, just like in those days when I had quit my job, when I didn't have a job, and didn't want a job. I would leave the house in the morning to look for a job, and I would go to the library and return without a job, but with a new understanding of the world. I finished many half-read books in the reading room for which candy wrappers, sewing threads, apple stems, and tissues served as bookmarks. I collected them with care and brought them home, with the intention of creating a room of keepsakes of the books I had read. Now my mind is on a room of keepsakes for all my half-read books. Maybe in an hour I'll start reading an epic and let the dawn be victorious, just like in those days when I had a job and read until the first rays of sun shone, when I worked a lot and read even more, when, in that time, I could carve a silhouette sitting by the window with eyes riveted on a page.

Whatever I've read I've read.

I've read to live on, remembering the reader.

Memories of the Reader: this is my new, atypical title, and I'm trying to remember all the images and sentences that were once his feelings. I think about the reader for days and don't understand why I inhale his absence in pain, why I can't live in part, why guilt appears with a yarn of incompleteness. Why do I suddenly feel embarrassed when I'm talking to people, and why do I eat directly in front of my library, sadly caressing the covers of my books? I don't want to surrender. I'm trying to weld all my passages together, drop everything in the middle of the day, run home, and open up a book again:

"But sometimes when I was starting a new story and I could not get it going, I would sit in front of the fire and squeeze the peel of the little oranges into the edge of the flame and watch the sputter of blue that they made."[3]

And the book closes and nothing comes out and the squeezed juice of the peel of the little oranges sputters in the fire and the flame flares up in blue and thought loses its meaning and the tongue works without a subject and memory is merely one sentence and gesture a meeting.

The lights of lampposts pour down from the street like thick drops from a candle. The names of the books stacked around my bed change every day, but none are ever opened. I can't sleep. Now I have to wait until dawn and dream that the incompleteness on the other side of my window will irreversibly abandon me, when birds will circle in this mysterious expanse and yield to the swift rolls of the wind while I scatter with the feathers, bequeathing my final passage to freedom.

According to Roland Barthes, when we kill an author, we give birth to ourselves as readers.[4] *By contrast, when we breathe life*

[3]Ernest Hemingway, *A Moveable Feast*, 1964.

[4]Roland Barthes, "The Death of the Author," *Norton Anthology of Theory and Criticism*, gen. ed.

into an author, we presume that possessing information about the author is essential to our interpretation of the text we are reading. In other words, we give the author authority over our interpretation of the text, and by doing so, we kill ourselves as readers.

Unlike readers, however, who can choose to kill or breathe life into an author, translators have traditionally been expected to be mouthpieces of the author. In John Dryden's words, a translator ought to "perfectly comprehend the genius and sense of his author, the nature of the subject, and the terms of the art or subject treated of."[5] *If a translator is caught with even the slightest "error" in translation, he or she is frequently judged for it, and sometimes very harshly: "The Pilgrim's Progress, the only book in our language which rivals Robinson Crusoe in popularity, has failed to produce any effect in Portugal. This is the translator's fault; for never was book more cruelly mutilated."*[6]

With the rise of literary criticism as an academic discipline, we have come to understand that interpretation is not the work of one authority informing us of what a text means. Rather, interpretation is only one point of view through a myriad of windows that continuously change over time. Yet, translators are still expected to somehow have superior knowledge over a text: they are expected to justify their interpretation and the choices they made in their translation. And depending on who reads their translation, the criticism will be leveled with the reader's

---

Vincent B. Leitch, W.W. Norton & Company, 2001. 1470.

[5]John Dryden, "On Translation," *Theories of Translations*, eds. Rainer Schulte and John Biguenet, University of Chicago Press, 1992. 31.

[6]Article III, "Extractos em Portuguez e em Inglez; com as Palavras Portuguezas propriamente accentuadas, para facilitar o Estudo d'aquella Lingoa," *The Quarterly Review* (Volume 1, May 1809), 249.

expectations. Does the reader expect the translation to be accurate and read fluently? What if the original didn't read fluently? What if accuracy is a subjective interpretation?

If we agree that it is impossible for a translator to be a mouthpiece of the author, then we must also agree that translation is nothing more than one possible interpretation of a text and that a translator should have the liberty of "killing an author." In my experience, however, breathing at least some life into an author has been a useful tool. Meeting with the author I was translating, Aram Pachyan, helped shape my interpretation of his texts. Researching material on a dead author like Aksel Bakunts helped me get a more nuanced grip on his stories.

Despite its advantages, it is nonetheless fair to be critical of the notion of "breathing life into an author." One might, for instance, question the level of interference of an author. How much authority should an author be given over the translation of their work? Should an author be allowed to interfere unsolicited? Should a translator always have access to an author or material about the author? And is there a measurable difference in a translation between those translators who "breathed life into an author" and those who "killed an author"?

Answers to these questions may radically differ between text and translator. My best response, as a translator, is to indiscriminately take in all the tools available, but only selectively choose those that are the most useful for any particular text.

Nairi Hakhverdi

BOGHOS KUPELIAN

"Black and White Moments"

(fiction)

Translated by Tamar Boyadjian

The socially unjust reality of a country full of rich diamond mines was that from an early age, the black girls—sometimes even with breasts not fully developed—would take their womanhood to the streets.

In order to secure a living for their families, they were forced to give up their young and innocent bodies to those willing to pay the price. For the most part these were wealthy black men and white foreigners. The heroine of this story belongs to this group of girls.

Among the women of the upper class in Africa, it was quite possible to come across true *pozes*. The rest were poor girls, young in age. In the region—having spent their entire childhood half naked and starving, illiterate and unlearned—the only way left to earn a living for these girls was to sell their bodies. No opposition from their parents. On the contrary, they would encourage their young daughters in this direction. And the money they collected bit-by-bit, instead of spending on costume jewelry or clothes of the latest fashion—they would empty into the palms of Lebanese merchants. Perhaps this was the case because the Lebanese themselves—also naked and barefoot as children preferred to "dress well," despite the oppressive heat and sweat of their country.

Eomi was different from her friends. She liked to be one man's "girl." She tried to remain as faithful as she could to him. Eomi had a heart, one of those hearts capable of loving. Her fate had cast her to the streets, in filth. In her youth—just like the daughters of her rich neighbors—she also dreamed of becoming a wife, having children, being a mother. She had ripped out the entire magazine for its fashion pictures, of newlywed couples, those with pictures of bridal gowns on mannequins, and she had decorated the walls of her tiny room with these advertisements.

A Lebanese merchant had taken her virginity. He had been a good friend of her father . . . And as soon as Eomi had returned from *Bondo*—the secret female circumcision society—the Lebanese, married and with children, had paid a large sum of money to Eomi's father and had taken her by car to a secret place, where he had housed her. Despite her young age, Eomi was to find all this quite natural. In a way, she was much happier in the house of the Lebanese man. She would dress well, eat well, and sleep on a soft bed. But those days did not last long. The honeymoon was very short . . .

The Lebanese man became distant after a while, and lost interest. Sometimes there were days where he wouldn't even show up, almost forgetting Eomi even existed. One day, he showed up with a friend, drunk. Eomi was not pleased by his lustful gaze. They continued to drink. The newcomer started feeling up different parts of the girl's body. And rather than her Lebanese "husband" objecting to the matter, it seemed as though he was actually getting pleasure from it. A little later, claiming he had to go work, he left Eomi to the gaze of this lustful man.

From that day forward, Lebanese men would come and go. Sure, they would bring gifts or leave money when they left. But this was not what Eomi understood by "marriage." One day, an unmannerly Lebanese man over-poured his cup. And after acting like a savage towards the girl, he proposed unspeakable things, beating Eomi in a horrifying manner. She collected her things and ran away to a friend's house in the city. If she had gone back to her father, he would have returned her right back to the Lebanese after beating her. Her father would have honored his word . . .

Eomi was mature, well beyond her age—her eyes had been opened. She had no other way out but to turn to the streets with her friend's guidance. But if a girl has individuality, if she has a natural intelligence, has a heart, certainly one day what is deserving will come. And it happened, just that way.

A Lebanese man who had just arrived in Africa fell madly in love with Eomi. She had already grown taller, her figure fuller; she had been bestowed with a certain feminine beauty. And she had taken charge of the girls like her, the ones on the streets.

The Lebanese man returned home for vacation. He came back with a pretty wife from Zahlé. Without even saying a word, Eomi silently disappeared from the man's life. She loved the man, but she also had the spiritual greatness to accept the realities of life. In the meantime, the Lebanese bridegroom was impotent for months. He could not get an erection from the white-skinned nakedness of his bride. And, as he confessed, he could only find the strength and ability after dreaming of Eomi. He would make love to Eomi in his mind.

After separating from the Lebanese, she moved on to a series of Europeans. A year or two; and then they would return to where they came from, certainly taking a piece of Eomi's soft and sentimental heart with them. What remained with the girl was a handful of photographs, as a memory; they would be placed on the wall to enlarge the already existing series of prior heroes.

Then, after some time she was in a terrible accident. The others—those who were in the car with her—died; she stayed alive. It is as though the huge scar on her face had come to take something away from her feminine charm. Regardless of the fissure on her face, she was able to queue up European suitors, back to back . . . They would say that Eomi had such an enrapturing female energy, such a warm charm, that she would enslave the men. However, she preferred to reverse the roles in their favor.

It was a hot, suffocating day. After finishing up my work in the city, I decided to go to the City Hotel for a cold beer. This antique hotel had become a common meeting place for the country's intelligentsia and *pozes*. It was the only site in town that still preserved something of the past. It was one of my past loves, and perhaps also because one my favorite novelists, Graham Greene, had lived there thirty years prior and written his astonishing novel on the upper terrace. After him, everything had remained the same. The furniture, the bar, the atmosphere, even the people . . .

Sitting in the corner, I was examining those present. The unapproachable faces of the unfamiliar women. An acquaintance—an editor, in fact—directed himself towards the jukebox with a young girl. After putting in a handful of money, he walked away cursing. The girl remained there alone.

A well-known surgeon, who at the same time was also a well-known drunkard, yelled from his corner, "Now he will go and publish a raging review of the jukebox in his newspaper . . ." And he laughed out loud, full of breath. The girl called me by name. Beautiful as a deer, she had large eyes. She smiled. She was pretty, and she knew it. She was expecting me to call her over to my table. She was a new, unfamiliar face. She was in white shoes with long stiletto heels, beautiful white trousers. Her skin had a lighter color. Clearly, she belonged to the Susu tribe. It may be that she did not know I was married. Anyway, that was not important for them. Apart from that, I loathe love that can be bought.

The girl approached. It is as though she has intended not to leave her prey astray. Hopefully from the way I looked over at her, she came to a different conclusion. It was not for false modesty; I just wanted to be alone. If only she knew how much she reminded me of my heroine, Eomi. She is not present. She could not be present. But when I enter the bar of this hotel, she becomes more alive than the people there. As if she were a celestial being. The reality, the grotesqueness of this world; she could not be a part of it.

She approaches, sits next to me with pleasure, coquettishly. Such a familiar seat to her, where the heat of her body would delay. The pictures, one after another, would come to life again.

* * *

It was upon my return from Lebanon, after a long absence. A drink. She approached me with a glass of beer in her hand. I don't know how to define our friendship. No physical contact, we had no such relationship in all those years. Was it pity? Fascination? Or just pure curiosity.

She came and sat next to me.

"How was Europe?" I asked.

"I didn't go to Europe. I haven't left the city in over a year."

"Then where have you been hiding?"

"I wasn't in hiding. Didn't you hear what happened?"

I hadn't heard. My absence from the city had been long lasting. The other problems in my life, I had other headaches to deal with. She didn't give me a chance to respond.

"I was in a serious engagement with a Dutch civil engineer."

She paused for a moment. Her face inviting me to tell her more. One night, just like this—by chance, we met one another.

And what was intended to be a single meeting for one evening, later turned into a strong bond of love. She was the engineer's first African. He had not believed his eyes . . . He had asked, begged, to spend the next evening with her. And just like this, months had flown by.

". . . your lover was most definitely a bachelor," I said, interrupting the impetus of her speech.

"No, that was precisely the misfortune."

The man was married to a fair Dutch beauty. Their constant arguments had broken the foundations of their marriage. She had packed her bags and returned to Holland for winter sports with a former lover. In his loneliness, the man had jumped into Eomi's lap to find solace. And shortly after, not used to the climate of Africa, he had caught malaria. Eomi could not leave him alone. She had taken care of him, night and day. She had cooked for him, cleaned for him, and had attended to the needs of this abandoned Dutch man; she has managed to save him from the fangs of death. The president of the man's company had written to his wife. She had left her winter sport almost half-way, returning to attend to her sick husband . . .

His wife's behavior had strengthened his ties further to the African "street girl." They had begun to expose their once curtained relationship—*to go public*. In his eyes, this was the least he could do to reward the girl's sacrifice. And for an African *poz*, there could be nothing more touching, no gift more valuable that could ever be imagined. To have a white lover, and to be "saved" by him was in and of itself a grace. And so like this? Hand-in-hand, to walk around freely . . . Atlantic Club, Tropicana, an Armenian restaurant. To dine, to drink, to dance. The powerful influence it left on the other women of the streets was stupefying . . .

The wife from Holland suddenly changed her mind. Tired of all the different varieties of winter sports, she decided to return to her husband. With an old, cheap bag in her hand, Eomi was forced to depart. Eomi made a particular effort, but she could not hold her tears back. Lost in heavenly reckoning, they were just flowing. Eomi felt herself deeply connected to this European engineer. And she was terrified of giving a proper name to that feeling. Nature always somehow mixes a sense of *fatalism* with love. Perhaps one would be incomplete without the other . . .

But they continued to see one another in secret. These precipitous meetings didn't carry the sweetness of their former life. Eomi complies. She wants to return to the City Hotel, but surprisingly that life is not appealing to her anymore. Eomi is startled by the thought of sitting on another man's lap.

"So you left the life of the streets," I interrupted, without being able to resist my satisfaction. "It was time for you to be attached to someone in a serious way." I didn't use the word marriage. In black Africa, when a couple cohabitates, they are considered married, in a natural way. She moved her shoulder.

"Although my boyfriend does not tend to my needs as he should, I try not to give into temptation . . . the poor man has a demanding wife, you know?" It is as though she read my mind; she hesitated for a second, and then she explained, "I simply came to the hotel today to meet my friends. I told myself, let me go have a drink, change my mood." And emphatically—as though she was communicating good news—she continued, "let me not forget to mention that as husband and wife they are perpetually arguing. The madam feels she's been reproached. Rather than a black woman, if her husband had cohabitated with a white woman, she might not have been so upset. The Dutch wife might have just been a little jealous."

This meeting of ours was to be the last.

His Dutch wife did not have an opportunity to complain for long. The engineer took Eomi in and sent his wife to Holland to engage in winter sports . . .

The Europeans were left with their mouths open; they scoffed at the man for his insult to the white color. Everything was excusable for the European, as long a black speck was not cast on their godly whiteness . . .

He fell because of his friends. They turned their backs on him. He was let go at his job. The president of the bank began to create problems for him.

These consecutive problems somehow made him even more tenacious. He suffered. He found a job in an African company. They continued to live together; he loved Eomi. He wanted to have a child with her. Eomi stopped taking the pill. With different forms of medication and care, she tried to make herself fertile. She was not successful; she was disappointed. Impotent, she turned herself over to the care of a village "doctor." She had made it her life's work to give the man she loved a child. The other—the Dutch woman—was infertile. Perhaps, with her limited understanding she believed that with the birth of a child, she would cleanse her female organs, and rid them of the stains of being a *poz* . . . She was attempting the impossible.

After the enormous loss of blood, Eomi never found herself again. In the lap of her white lover, she surrendered her last breath to his teary gaze . . .

Translating any work from its original form into not only a different language, but a different world, is a herculean task. As someone who grew up in the world Raymond Boghos Kupelian—my father—experienced in Sierra Leone, West Africa, I can say that context is everything. This was Sierra Leone in the sixties and seventies. People thought a bit differently then, and had a distinctive set of values and cultural understandings. You had to be there to really get it. The story is also written in the author's own Western Armenian: one of the oldest recorded languages still being spoken—which in itself is richly descriptive. A literal translation would simply hinder the intent of the words and paragraphs and make them unreadable. (Shakespeare, for example, was actually written in English, yet one has to perform it, not merely read it, to truly understand it). The task of the translator then is skillfully varied: moving from Armenian to English, portraying an era quite distinct from today, being mindful of a culturally sensitive world with all its intricacies, yet respecting the very heart and soul of the writer himself. In essence, this is not much different from Lord Byron pouring over ancient Armenian and Persian texts on the island of St. Lazarus in Venice, Italy. So when such a story is told, the translator must find a way to encapsulate the journey to a different audience. Only a writer may undertake a task like that, and a translator such as Tamar M. Boyadjian, has met that challenge here.

Roger Kupelian, Writer, Director, Filmmaker

VAHAN ISHKHANIAN

"Family Album: Vardanush," from the documentary novel, *Those Large, Blue Eyes*

(fiction)

Translated by Dzovinar Derderian

1937

October 8th

My mother, Biurakn, is ten years old.

I don't know if it was November or December. Usually I would sleep soundly, but this time something woke me up. I jumped out of bed. It must have been 2 a.m. My mom, all pale, was standing by the door. Lisa was crying. My grandmother was pounding her knees. Two or three chekists[1] were turning the room upside-down. There was also a woman with them. She had blue eyes and a stern face. She was terrifying. She was patting down my mother. My poor mother! What could possibly be on her in the middle of the night? I don't know.

I felt that they were going to take my mother away. I started to scream. They were telling me, "Girl jan,[2] don't cry, your mother will come back tomorrow." I said, "I know that if you take her, she will never come back."

I was running behind the car, barefoot, in my nightgown. I don't know how they brought me back home.

The chekists took away with them all the tiny-little presents that I had received for my birthday, like my gilded earrings and spoons; they took all those with them. They took some of the books too, and they piled the rest in the courtyard and ordered to burn them. Lisa and my grandmother also burned the books.

---

[1]Members of the Extraordinary Commission for Combatting Counterrevolution and Sabotage in the Soviet Union.

[2]"Jan," which is an endearing word used in Armenian, Persian and Turkish.

I didn't go to school for a few days. I lay on the taht[3] thinking that since they took my mother away I have no right to live; it is better if I die. But I didn't die.

Then upon their insistence, I pulled myself together and went to school. On a large board on the wall were the pictures of all the "A" students. My picture was no longer there. As the daughter of the people's enemy, they had removed my picture.

They removed us from our home. They threw us—me, my maternal uncle (Vardkes), my uncle's wife, Lisa, and their newborn daughter Minush—in a little room that was partially underground.

At school, I would notice that the moment those in the higher grades would see me they would murmur to each other, saying that "she is Vahan Cheraz's daughter, they arrested her mother, they took out gold from their homes with meshoks."[4] I can remember all of that so clearly.

One day, I was sitting in class, and during our lesson, the door opened and that woman–the one who had come to take my mother away—she looked inside, with her large, blue eyes. I was horrified. I was on pins and needles! She waved her hand to the teacher, and Yesayan Hasmik from our class went out. During the break I asked Hasmik:

"Hasmik, who was that?"

"She's my mother," she said.

"What's her name?"

[3]Persian for bed.

[4]Here the word used for bag was "meshok" in Russian.

"Nvard."

"It's Nvard Yesayan?"

"Yeah."

I broke off my relations with that Hasmik.

1896

Vardanush Andreasian was born in the Western Armenian province of Kharbert[5] in the village of Hazar[6] next to the town of Chmshkatzag.[7] Her mother's name was Iskuhi, her father's—Aleksan.

1915

The Turks kill Vardanush's first husband—Boghos Zenneyan. By then Vardanush's two-year-old son had died.

The Zazas of Kharbert save Vardanush's family from her native Hazar village, by hiding them in the mountains.

1916-1917

In Karin (Erzurum) Vardanush meets her future husband—Vahan Cheraz—who was working for an organization that was named "Armenian Headquarters" dealing with refugee affairs.

October

Vardanush and Vahan Cheraz get married. A few months later Vahan is exiled to Siberia.

---

[5]Currently Harput in Turkey.

[6]Currently Anıl in Turkey.

[7]Present-day Çemişgezek in Turkey.

1926

February 24

Here's the news that you wanted to hear. Vahan was already freed from his exile. He doesn't want to return here for now because of the horrific cold weather, because his health has deteriorated, which is very concerning. Secondly, he's now convinced that it is necessary to leave here. I'm trying to find means to move our dear ones to other places. There is hope for success. In that case, we may need some money for the road.

Respectfully,

Vardanush Cheraz

My address is Vardanush Cheraz Poligon Leninakan,[8] Armenia.

1927

January 25

My mother Biurakn is born. Vahan Cheraz, her father, is keeping a diary of Biurakn. Here is a portion from "The Annals of Biurakn."

"Biurakn was born at 5:15 p.m. in the American hospital of the 'Kazachi Post' area.[9] Vardanush did not suffer much, and gave birth without a doctor or midwife. The little one is thin. She weighs only 6.5 pounds."

---

[8] Leninakan was the Soviet-era name for Gyumri.

[9] "Post" here signifies a military observation position. "Kazachi Post" signifies an area in Gyumri.

June 23

Vahan Cheraz is arrested.

October 10

From Vardanush's letter to her brother Vazken Andreasian in Paris

"Don't worry for us my sweet *janik*.[10] We have hope that this too shall pass. It's been a few days that I have returned from Tiflis. I saw Vahan. He seemed to be in a good mood. We hope that within a month the misunderstanding will be resolved."

1928

January 9 (according to the document)

They shoot Vahan Cheraz.

May 10

Vardanush's letter to Paris, to her mother Iskuhi

My dear destitute mother. What news do you expect? Didn't you understand the reason why I've been silent? Couldn't you conclude that I am still the same unfortunate person I always was? With the only exception that now I have a loving child, who means everything to me; she gives me life, even though I am the one who gave her life.

Just know that I would have felt the same grief. Moreover, mother, if I had refused him . . . since I had already known him, that was enough. At least now my conscience is clear. I

[10] Here *janik* is a diminutive of *jan*.

did the right thing not to refuse him. Being conscious of this consoles me a lot. If I had done the opposite, what would have consoled me now? Finally, now I am a mother, and to what a child! One should see her to know what kind of a treasure this innocent angel is. My grief is that my little baby had every right to enjoy her exceptional father, who has been a father to others. I become bitter when I ask myself why my dearest little one should face such an irreplaceable loss.

I can't accept this. Otherwise, believe me, for me it's all the same; it's not something new. It's not new that I will feel unfortunate. Especially that now I am going forward with this awareness that I have to protect my health at every cost, so that I can take care and caress the two Biurakn-s of my memories [in other words 'the two sources of my memories'].[11] It seems to me that I have two consignments with me left from two loved ones: one is an unprotected child and the other an old child,[12] for whom it is really worth living. And believe me, this loss makes me more aware of my new responsibilities, gives me strength to endure every misfortune. I surprise myself. Is it me who is still living? Believe me, I am living with more humility, patience, and I have a greater will to live. I feel healthier." My dear mother, I know I have been the cause for all of your agony and pain, but know my dear, that I had committed no sin to have such an end; forgive me my kind and gentle mother for having given you so much sorrow unwillingly; when I think that way I am terrified. If you love me, don't darken your, my

[11]Here the author is playing with the word and name Biurakn, which while being the name of her daughter, also means "of thousands of sources."

[12]By "old child" she means the wife of her previous husband Poghos Zennean's brother. Her name was Narduhi Zennean. In the letters she is often referred to as grandmother.

father, and brother's days. It doesn't bring any good. If you think the way I do, you will not cry that much. Believe me I did not cry at the time of the unheard of catastrophe; maybe I am insensitive as the grandmother says. Although I have not filled out the applications for Vardkes to leave for Constantinople, because I was not in the mood, but I am sure that he will succeed, and if Vardkes ends up in your hands, don't you ever agree to separate from your two sons at any cost! It's enough how much you suffered from longing, my conscience torments me a lot knowing that my loved ones have suffered with me against my will, that I have always wanted to make my parents the happiest in the world, because they are worthy of it, that's the thought that angers me. Finally, it's enough, don't suffer for me, consider that I have gone on exile and died. Aren't we Armenian as well, which Armenian mother doesn't have her child's anguish in her heart? Poor Nono[13] was probably not expecting this (and who would have expected it). He has just come to his senses, the last senses of an Armenian they say. This time let him ask for an explanation, for what? Oh, it's enough.

Biurakn Cheraz

They would keep my father's large picture wrapped up, on top of the cupboard. When nobody was at home, I would slowly climb up on a chair, and with difficulty would take the picture from the top of the cupboard. I would unwrap it, admire it, and put it back in its place.

* * *

[13]Nono was Vahan Cheraz's father, Gaspar Cheraz (1850-1928), who lived in Constantinople.

Biurakn Cheraz

My mom must have thought that I was some kind of super child. She took me to ballet classes, to piano classes. She would attend to my drawing. She had given me the freedom to roam around whenever I wanted. I would bring home stray cats and dogs. I would catch little newborn frogs and bring them home. She would throw a party for my birthday and invite all my girlfriends. She would sew for them the same dress as she would sew for me. She had sewn the same dress for Jemma, Silva, and me.

My mother would sew for me different costumes of Eskimos, Ukrainians, Kurds, and Norwegians. In these costumes of different peoples I would dance at the kindergarten performances. They would take us on promenades; they would give us clay, and we would make different things with the clay.

My mother was an accountant at the state theater. I would always go and sit in the theater hall and watch actors practice. Every time the circus was in town, my mother would take me to see it. I knew that I would either become a circus performer or an actress.

Our weekly visits to the bath were a festivity. We would go with a carriage, with gathered *bohças*,[14] with food, with the entire family, by scrubbing each other's backs; sometimes they would call a *kisaci*.[15] There was a clay mine near Gyumri. Women would wash their hair with that clay; the clay-water would always flow on the floor.

---

[14]"Bokhcha," in Turkish *Bohça*, is used here meaning bundle.

[15]Here the word "keseci" is used which comes from the Turkish word *keseci*—the one who cleans people by scrubbing them with a rough scrub mitt called *kese*. The Armenian transliteration is "kisaci."

I remember my mother, with her black hair spread out, sitting majestically.

As long as my mother was there, I had an amazing childhood.

1937

June 3

Vardanush's letter to her brother Vazken

From now on, look for Vahan and Vardanush in Biurakn.

December 26

Portions from the decision of the ASSR SS (Secret Service) trio

They heard

The Armenian SSR [Soviet Socialist Republic] NKVD[16] of the Lenkagh [Leninakan city] Department N. 1470, conviction of Cheraz Vardanush Aleksanovna, born in 1895, inhabitant of Leninakan, from a large merchant family.

She is convicted for being an active member of the Dashnak[17] organization, and has maintained ties with their foreign bureau. Her husband was shot for being the leader of the scouting organization in Armenia; he occupied with recruiting new members for the Dashnak organization. He had ties with Iran, whence the wife of an influential Dashnak came

[16]The "People's Commissariat for Internal affairs," which was the main Soviet secret service force in the 1930s and 1940s.

[17]"Dashnak" refers to the Armenian Revolutionary Federation (*Hay Heghapokhakan Dashnaktsutiun*)—a political party established in 1890.

to visit him. He was maintaining contact with Dashnaks in foreign countries.

They decided

Cheraz Vardanush Aleksanovna: to be shot, her property to be confiscated.

Biurakn Cheraz as a ten-year-old: that little girl and her old grandmother holding hands.

I was a ten-year-old girl and with my grandmother we were going from the prison to the Cheka,[18] from the Cheka back to the prison so that we could take food to my mother. I would go to the prison, stand in line, when my turn would come they would say: there is no one like that here, go to the Cheka, my turn would come they would say she is not here. So I was never able to get my mother anything.

With a two-month delay I received an envelope from my mother. She was asking for warm clothes. We went to the prison; they said that she is no longer in Leninakan. I would write many letters and in response would be told that the trio has convicted her to a ten-year exile without the right of any written communication. Later I heard from a woman who was freed from the Yerevan prison, that she was killed in one of Yerevan's prisons.

1938

I was a kid, eleven years old; I went to the home of the chief of the KGB. They had shown me the place. I went up to

[18]Cheka was an emergency committee existing in many cities during the Soviet era.

the second floor, knocked at the door. They opened. I asked, where my mother was, why did you take her away, and I started crying. He didn't say anything; he was looking at me sternly. I was so humiliated.

Biurakn Andreasian, 11 years old

My uncle's wife Liza was worried about my last name being Cheraz. She had a friend in Gyumri's registration office, and got a paper that showed that they had adopted me. I became Biurakn Andreasian, daughter of Vardkes.

1958

October 27

"Secret. Decision of Armenia's SSR (Soviet Socialist Republic):

Examined the complaint of the deputy prosecutor of ASSR in the court session, against the decision of the former trio 26/12 of the ASSR SS (Secret Service), with which she has been convicted to the maximum level of punishment, condemned to be shot: Vardanush Cheraz of Aleksan, born in 1895, in Turkey, she lived in Leninakan, an Armenian . . .

[. . .]

Cheraz's case was examined as a serious violation of the law, her arrest by the prosecutor is not permitted, there is no charge, the case has not been opened, translators have not been invited, the truth of the operating information does not seem reliable.

According to the information of the case and its complementary examination, the charges made against Cheraz are not justified.

The judicial council decided to abridge the case that charged Vardanush Cheraz, since the charges had not been proven.

1962

Biurakn Andreasian

My mother was an accountant. The last place she had worked in was the bread factory. When they recognized she was innocent, they gave her a salary for her last three months. To be honest, I didn't want to take it. Then I thought, oh, whatever, I might as well? I will buy her grandchild a present on behalf of my mother. Avo[19] was seven years old. He was going to start school and with that money we went to Leningrad[20] with Avo.

[19]Avo is one of Biurakn's sons.

[20]Now St. Petersburg in Russia.

I have translated what is already a work of translation. In this piece, Vahan Ishkhanian selected letters and documents, then organized them in a particular order and connected the different people and places appearing in the text. What is more, he altered and standardized the spelling of the original sources. With his translation he aimed to tell a personal story meant to evoke emotion, and here I have selected fragments from Ishkhanian's narrative and provided my version of them.

The text called to me as a woman because of Ishakhnian's bold positioning of his female protagonists; as I selected fragments of the text I further focused on the female voice. The rich archival sources on a rather obscure period of Armenian history and Ishakhanyan's creative use of them appealed to the historian in me. Ishkhanian's translation highlights his family history but it also includes notes of the history of Stalinism, of the Armenian genocide, of relations between the Diaspora and Soviet Armenia, as well as a history of trauma.

If a historian approached the same archival material first hand, she would try to translate a historical process. For example, she would examine the variation of spellings and language appearing in the texts to understand how quickly or slowly citizens like Vardanush adopted, contributed to, or resisted Soviet-era language policies. Such a historical narrative would require a different sequence of the archival material (letters, documents and oral accounts), which would hide the emotional world revealed through Ishkhanian's translation.

I visualize Ishkhanian's text as a museum, with a selection of art on display, with no interpretation or contextualization. Thus, the spectators, left to their own senses and knowledge, are forced to imagine the feelings that Vardanush may have had, the images that she described, the feelings and experiences that she had but did not verbalize—everything left undissected for the audience. The readers are also left to situate this narrative in their historical knowledge and memory. In this sense, and unlike the work of most historians, Ishkhanian's testimony leaves room for further interpretation and, ultimately, other forms of translation.

In this sense, translation allows one to see details, thus it allows the historian to interpret a text more deeply. The minutiae of a text unravels itself when one attempts to translate and at moments when the translator faces impasses. Translating the above narrative allowed me to come face to face with the historical actors' multilingual world, one so deeply adopted by the Armenian language that such cultural influences pass unawares. Indeed, I had to consult Russian, Turkish, Persian, and Armenian dictionaries in the course of this translation.

My experience in translating this excerpt highlights the value of historiography in different languages and the importance of turning to literary translations when writing about cultural, linguistic, and emotive layers embedded in our material and symbolic formations of history. In this sense, reflecting on the processes of selecting, sequencing, structuring as well as the translator's subjectivity as part and parcel of the process of translation allows one to detect what is hidden and what is revealed through different types of translations.

Dzovinar Derderian

MARC NICHANIAN

"Still Born: Repetition, Translation, And Translatability"

(Lecture, University of Michigan)

I.

What I will try to present in this lecture belongs to the oldest layer of my long inquiry into Zareh Vorpouni's work. First, a few words on the general context and then on Vorpouni and his production as a novelist, which will certainly not be superfluous. We need to recall that, before 1915, the novel was a genre largely neglected in the Western Armenian literary tradition; only the so-called Realist school had begun to cultivate it. The novel is the genre of duration. Before 1915, in the nightmare of death, the organ of duration had atrophied, as Hagop Oshagan says.[1]In the Diaspora, in contrast, the novel experienced an extraordinary flowering. We also need to recall that 1930 was a pivotal year for the Armenian novel in the Diaspora, for, from 1926 to 1934, Oshagan composed all his novels, in particular his groundbreaking *Mnatsortats* [*The Remnants*]; Costant Zarian published his *Pancoop yev mamout'i voskornerë* [*The Pancoop and the Bones of the Mammouth*] (1932); Shahan Shahnour released the famous Diasporan novel *Nahanj arrants' yergi* [*Retreat Without Song*] (1929).[2] That same year, Vorpouni published *P'ordzë* [*The Attempt*], the first novel in the cycle *The Persecuted*. In this same period, even Nigoghos Sarafian was writing novels, *Khakhiskhen her-*

[1]On Hagop Oshagan (1883-1948), see my book, *Le Roman de la Catastrophe*, Geneva: MétisPresse, 2008. The most explicit passage where Oshagan mentions the "violence" to which the Western-Armenian writers were subjected because the "organ of duration" had atrophied in them is found in his *Hamapatker* [Panorama of Western-Armenian literature], vol. V (Jerusalem, 1952), p. 153. For a French translation of that passage, see *Le Roman de la Catastrophe*, p. 136.

[2]An (incorrect) English translation of *Nahanjë* is available, Shahan Shahnur, *Retreat without song*, trans. Mischa Kudian, London: Mashtots Press, 1972. A French translation has recently been released, Armen Lubin (Chahan Chahnour), *La Retraite sans fanfare*, wrongly subtitled *Histoire illustrée des Arméniens à leur arrivée à Paris suite au génocide de 1915-1916*, translated under the direction of Krikor Beledian (Paris: L'ACTEMEM, 2009).

ru [*Far from Base*], *T'omas Aypanelin* [*Thomas the Blameworthy*], and in book form, *Ishkhanuhin* [*The Princess*]. In 1934, Hratch Zartarian published *Mer Keank'ë* [*Our Life*].

These three titles—*The Retreat, The Attempt, Our Life*—belonging to three different authors, form a compact ensemble: they are indiscernible, as if they were three different articulations of the same set of problems. There are, to begin with, the external similarities in the basic situation depicted with their narratives: a young generation arrives in France where it has to face the reality of permanent exile and learn the ways of its foreign environment. These novels were, indeed, read for more than one generation as realist works. One can, taking them the other way around, trace the way the Foreign is inscribed in them, both as a category and as an experience. Vorpouni, before all, would carry the experiment as far as possible in his later work. This aspect of the novels of 1930 failed to emerge in the early, realist readings. In subsequent years, Beirut's cultural influence reinforced the initial misperception. Only with the appearance in 1964 of Zareh Vorpouni's *Yev yeghev mard* [*And There Was Man*] was that influence in some way neutralized. This novel worked something of a revolution in Armenian letters. If it had been widely read, it could have enabled the youngest generation of the Diaspora to attain its proper identity, to find its own way. I say this in the conditional. The reality is that it was too late for such discoveries and revolutions. And, nevertheless, this novel of Vorpouni's counts, at least for my generation, as the most important event in the history of the Diaspora. It was hailed by H. Kurkjian as inaugurating a psychological turn in novelistic writing. But even more, what was at stake was an interrogation about how inaugural events were still possible in a domain in which duration had ceased to function. But who in the Diaspora was interested in this type of questions? Vorpouni's name remained widely ignored and his works are barely accessible today.[3]

Of the writers of the Paris school, Shahnour was the one who succeeded in capturing the attention of the age. There was a certain brio to his writing; he had, moreover, a knack for provoking his readers. He made a name for himself early on with his *Retreat.* The whole of his uprooted generation believed it had found its image in this novel, whose fame was cemented by a few controversial passages. Strangely enough, the success of the novel continues unabated to the present day. It has gone through at least three different editions in the Diaspora and two in (Soviet) Armenia. No other book has had comparable success among Armenians. Though the novel was widely read in France in the thirties, it quickly passed into the hands of the Eastern Diaspora—I mean, the Armenian speaking communities in the Middle East after 1950—where it won over new readers. This indicates one very precise thing: the novel was prized not because it depicted reality, but because it corresponded to the Armenian *representation* of that reality. Its readers were reading their own obsessive ideological representation in the novel, their own fear of and fascination for the Foreign. Shahnour's novel was as good at pandering to the fascination as it was at cultivating the obsession. In his "Second Equation," first published in the journal *Ahegan* (Beirut)

[3]On this generation of writers in exile, I refer the reader to Krikor Beledian's study, *Cinquante ans de littérature arménienne en France. Du même à l'autre*, Paris: CNRS, 2001.

in 1968, Harutiun Kurkjian engages with this point very well.[4] Of course there is more to say about Shahnour's treatment of the encounter with the Foreign. Yet, as long as the ideological overlay of fascination and obsession has not been stripped off, the rest will remain invisible.

The writer who made good on all of the promises of the generation of 1930 was Zareh Vorpouni. He was born in 1903. After a ruined adolescence and then three years at the Berberian School in Constantinople, he spent the rest of his life in France; his biography is intertwined with his ripening fiction. He conceived of the idea of writing a novelistic cycle with his first novel in 1929. The second work in the cycle, *T'egnatsun* [*The Candidate*], was not published until 1967, nearly forty years later. It was, at the time, necessitated by mourning; but it speaks volumes about the internal obstacles that were necessary to overcome in order to produce the novel of the Diaspora. One must also not forget the total isolation experienced by Vorpouni and his generation after WWII, the eclipse of Paris as a cultural rallying point for the Armenians, and the ascendency of Beirut. In any case, two other volumes were published in 1972 and 1974: *Asphaltë* [*Asphalt*] and *Sovorakan or më* [*A Day Like All the Others*].[5] The fifth volume remains unpublished. In 1982, the Paris journal *GAM* published what there was of the sixth volume. Between 1929 and 1964, Vorpouni also published several collections of short stories, which

[4] Harutiun Kurkjian, *Yerkrord havasarum pazmat'iv anhaytnerov* [Second Equation with multiple unknowns] has later been included in the book *P'ordz tara-grut'ean masin* [Essay on Writing Exile] (Paris: Collection "Diaspora arménienne", 1978), with a French translation.

[5] *Asphaltë* was released from the printhouse of the journal *Marmara* in Istanbul, in 1972, and subsequent references are cited from this edition. *Sovorakan or më* was released in Beirut by Sevan Publishing.

should be considered preparatory exercises for his major work. Vorpouni's novels have never seen the light of day in a way that would make them entirely accessible to readers. In my estimation, Vorpouni remains the most representative writer of the Diaspora.

In his 1967 novel, *The Candidate*, he offers a testimony—obviously an imagined one— in the middle of the novel. I cannot explain now the profundity and the subtlety of this gesture, which supposes or entails an interrogation about the secret limit between literature and testimony. This is for another time and a different lecture. Suffice to say that the novel revolves around the figure of a survivor, Vahakn, who, in a burst of madness, kills a Turkish friend, a student in Paris, who was apologizing, or God knows what—maybe he was asking for forgiveness. The main events of the novel are supposed to take place in 1927. Vahakn kills his Turkish friend, and, as a consequence, kills himself. In the time that elapses between the murder and the suicide, he writes a letter in which he explains his double gesture, a letter, more than fifty pages long, in the novel. He explains that he was already dead before the corpse of his friend; he then writes as a dead man, as the dead witness that he is, the absolute survivor. The letter is at the same time a testimony—the testimony of a survivor, an account of his particular experience of the Deportation. The letter shows that even if the main feature of the Paris writers was the encounter with the Other, the necessity of writing the Catastrophe and of re-experiencing or re-playing the limit of literature in the form of testimony was not absent from their preoccupations. Other survivors' accounts, the "real" ones, recount the sufferings, the death of the next of kin, the atrocities. They recount the Deportation. But they have nothing to say about the Catastrophe, if the Catastrophe is the death of the witness. How would they be able to bear witness for the death of the witness? One needs to be dead in order to bear witness. With this testimony of a survivor placed in the middle of a novel, and written by someone who is already dead, Vorpouni was, for the very first time, interrogating the intimate and conflicting relationship between literature and the testimonial account in general. With the enigmatic equivalence that Vorpouni established between murder and suicide, with his insistence on the necessity of cleaning ourselves from the poison that inhabits us—long before Hrant Dink—he invited his readers to reform themselves in order to open a way toward reconciliation, and to initiate the time of forgiveness. He was not understood. He was barely read. I will attend another time to the extraordinary subtlety of this treatment of testimony, which makes *The Candidate* one of the most powerful novels written in the Diaspora. It deserves a lecture entirely devoted to it. Today my topic is the third volume of the cycle, *Asphalt*.

At the center of this third volume there is what they call in Armenian *vizhum*, which can be "abortion" or "miscarriage." The oldest layer of my inquiry in Vorpouni's work is thus related to the event (the thoroughly novelistic event) of an aborted birth and consequently to the result of this aborted birth, a stillborn child as a figure. The aborted birth and the stillborn child appear in Vorpouni's novels relationally through a structure of repetition—I need to pause here first and, if possible, interpret or at the least comment. The structure of repetition is constantly present in Vorpouni's novels, with different modalities. One of these modalities is from novel to novel, the modified repetition of novelistic events that had already taken place, or had already been recounted, but now need to be recounted differently, the way a photographic image can be edited several times. The French word for "editing" in this case would be "*retoucher*." The second modality is stranger and much more disquieting. It's a question of repeating an event recounted in a different novel by a different author. In *Asphalt*, Nicole's death during childbirth can be read as a secret repetition of an event that itself was entirely inconspicuous at the end of Shahan Shahnour's *Retreat Without Song*. It could be, of course, a coincidence, or the result of an unconscious or very conscious rivalry between the two, as a result of which Vorpouni needed decades in order to rewrite Shahnour's successful novel, and to rewrite it in his own way, with his own categories.

In a very different context, it was no less strange when Blanchot was writing, in his own name and in the first person, an episode of Georges Bataille's "autobiography," as though it was his own. It is true that, in the case of the generation of Armenian writers gathered in Paris in 1930, there was a common experience, which can be subsumed under the title that I already referenced "The encounter with the Other," the Other being sometimes viewed as an alienating Other. And we will have to ask, then, in which form does this encounter take place, how are we to understand it, how is it recorded in literature? The third modality of repetition is the one that interests us here more closely and more immediately than the others. This time, it is indubitably a repetition, it is a repetition in the same novel, *Asphalt*. Something strange happens in that novel, not in the story that is recounted, or the scenes which are described. From pages 130 to 161 (in the only edition that we have at our disposal), the author has copied out what he had already written in the previous pages, sometimes word for word, sometimes taking liberties with the initial wording, and slightly modifying expressions or idiomatic phrases. I will give a few examples to illustrate my point, since I can't do more in the context of a lecture. But before doing so, I imagine that again it will not be superfluous to say a word about what happens in this third volume.

The novel recounts the relations between its main protagonist, Minas, and two French women, two sisters—Nicole and Monique. Minas has married Nicole and has eventually walked away from her. The story begins with a long scene of childbirth, which actually occupies the entire first half of the novel. The unborn child is understood to be Minas's child, although Minas never ceased to ask himself why Nicole fled his approaches. The riddle remains unresolved "even after the scene of the couch," which revealed to Minas the sexual closeness between the two sisters. The first half of the novel then places the reader in the room where, for a whole night, Nicole will fight death and Minas (who came back and took upon himself the responsibility of watching over her) will not move an inch to call the doctor. A large part of the novel is devoted to the analyses that Minas proposes to himself in order to explain and understand his failure, analyses that obviously are motivated by his sense of guilt. Intertwined with this long night-time scene we read day-time ones that describe the first meeting between Minas and Nicole, until the moment when in the early morning Monique arrives, Nicole is immediately sent to the hospital, and later the telephone rings, announcing Nicole's death. "The child had already died in the womb of its mother, doubtless well before Nicole was taken away . . ." And, again, mixed with these scenes are others that show from within the life of a leftist Armenian journal in Paris and the infighting between political parties that hate each other. The second part of the novel is devoted to Monique, with beautiful graphic descriptions of Minas engaging in sexual intercourse with her, intertwined with other scenes which in some way correspond to the general title of the novelistic series, where we see Minas running away through the streets of Paris.

Let us return to the question of repetition within the novel. As I noted earlier, beginning on page 130, and within the space of thirty pages, Vorpouni repeats through the same sentences, sometimes with a slightly different wording, what he had already written, modifying an idea here, a word there, with an imperceptible shift from the present to the past. Vorpouni simply returns to copying out sentences that he had already written in his manuscript and, in copying them or writing them a second time, changing their nature and status. It is possible to imagine that the duality of the sisters participates in the structure of repetition, and as a consequence that the same sentences have been written the first time in the sphere of Nicole, the second time in the sphere of Monique. The novel then separates sister from sister, since one of the novel's presuppositions (or of Minas's psychology) is the similitude of the sisters, their oneness, their proximity, their indestructible link, visible through their supposedly homosexual connection. The separation is then carried out in and through the novel. Minas was excluded from the Foreign. He had to recapture a lost territory. This was Vorpouni's way to regain control of the whole problematic concerning the encounter with the Foreign, which was the focus of the Paris group of novelists.

But this is only one way—a satisfying but not sufficient way—of interpreting the structure of repetition within the novel. Within the next novel in the series, the one published in 1974, *A Day Like All the Others*, Minas narrates a dream—it is a literary dream, to the extent that Nicole's death is repeated here (one more repetition) in the form of a dream, and this time it is clearly repeated as a murder. The literary dream doesn't need to be analyzed. It is itself the analysis of what happens in the fiction and as fiction. It repeats and it lays bare the novelistic project. In the dream the still born child enters the room, he's got a knife in the hand, he is heading toward Nicole who is lying on the couch, and he pushes the knife in her vagina. Here, for the first time, our murderer is revealed. It's the stillborn child. He had never shown up in the daylight before. If we recall the end of Shahnour's *Retreat,* Nénette was also transported to the hospital, covered in blood, but there was no explicit mention of a stillborn child. Here we are, at the end of Shahnour's novel: "And before all, before all, blood, blood everywhere. Blood on the bed and the floor, blood in several buckets filled with water, blood on rags, on shirts, on towels, blood even on the threshold of the house."[6] Was it a suicide, in accordance with the logic of the fiction? It's not clear. Or rath-

[6]*Nahanjë arrants' yergi*, p. 257 of the first edition.

er was it a miscarriage, an abortion? Here are Nénette's last words: "Pierrot, save me . . . This time, I swear . . . the doctor just confirmed, I swear . . . I am . . . I am really pregnant . . . Really pregnant . . ."[7] Yes, but again there is no mention of a stillborn child. And here, suddenly, in Vorpouni's novels, with Minas's dream, we know who committed this literary murder, provided that we read the novels through the grid of the structure of repetition. It is the stillborn child. He is on the stage, he comes into play, a knife in his hand. He proceeds toward the woman's naked body. He rips her belly open. The blood flows from the belly and the vagina, it spatters on the walls, it paints everything red: the rags, the shirts, the towels. Literary murders are cruel.

But who is this still born child? It is possible to read and to present him as a psychoanalytic figure? He lives in the innermost depths of the unconscious. But, in that case, whose unconscious? Can it be the same unconscious, from one author to the other? It is true that Freud himself hit hard with his Oedipus—again a figure, more than common—since Freud considered it as a common good or a common curse for the whole of humanity, as a constitutive element of our humanity after all? But, again, how are we to explain the fact that the Still Born Child manifests itself with the structure of repetition, with the implementation of that structure? And before all how are we to explain that its manifestation seems to be the central moment in the experience of the Foreign, the one that was the most profoundly hidden? The Still Born is here ; it lives, if I may say so -it is before our eyes, in the novelistic

[7]Ibid. p. 258.

dream. It was born as dead. In French they say, *un mort-né*. Born dead. Or prevented from being born. And the fact that he could not be born is equivalent in the novel with the reality of its being being deprived of a name. There is no name for it, for him or her, in language, and consequently in the dream. "I try to shout, to call, but I find no name to shout, while knowing very well that it is our child. It is a terrible thing not to know the name. Not to have a name. I want to shout its name. A borborygmus forms in my mouth, it grows to the point of explosion, to become a name, but it does not manage to make a name."[8]

Language here arrives at its limit. It experiments within itself, its own end, its own loss. Outside of literature, such an experience would be unconceivable, because it would need a language in order to be recorded and registered. I said earlier that the dream repeats and lays bare the novelistic project. Here is the project: to bring language to its limit, on the verge of its capacities, on the brink of its loss. It is at this point, on this borderline, there where a given language meets the Foreign, meets it own Other, it is here that the Still Born Child shows up, manifests itself, as a figure.

And upon this difficult understanding, we are confronted with a series of questions, which invite a new set of examinations. First, what does it mean for a language to meet the Foreign, to meet its own Other? Is it not true that every language, at some point, can meet with its own Other, and lose itself in the Foreign? Why then does not every language in the same way arrive to its own limit -in other words, to a point where it

---

[8]*Sovorakan or më*, p. 84.

disappears, in itself and for itself? "We have almost lost our language in the foreign," wrote Hölderlin two centuries ago. *Wir haben fast die Sprache in der Fremde verloren*. Was it the same experience as the one lived through by Vorpouni and transposed into words by him, not poetically but "novelistically"? Is it the case that German also, as a language, in and through Hölderlin's experience, had arrived to its end, to its limit, had met the Foreign, and had been lost, almost lost in the Foreign?

Second, we said earlier that here a language was experiencing its own limit and its own loss, its own disappearance, its own end. How can a language experience and record within itself its own loss, the loss of itself? This assertion reminds us of Georges Bataille's formulations about the inner experience, which is the experience of the loss of the subject, but which presupposes a subject that is able to experience its own loss, or at least is able to bear witness about that loss—a project which is apparently highly contradictory, and demands for a reflection on the nature of the survivor, the one who survives her own death, who survives the death of the witness within herself. Hence Maurice Blanchot's suggestion addressed to Bataille, which has remained unnoticed for a very long time—to carry out the inner experience as though he were the "last man," which clearly means the one who cannot be his own witness, a survivor.[9] The only question and difficulty then becomes

[9]See Georges Bataille, *Inner Experience*, trans. with an introduction by Leslie Anne Boldt, Albany: State University of New York Press, 1988, p. 61: "Blanchot asked me: why not pursue my inner experience as If were the last man? [. . .] The subject in experience loses its way, it loses itself in the object, which itself is dissolved. It could not, however, become dissolved to this point, if it's nature didn't allow it this change; the subject in experience in spite of everything remains [. . .] As the ancient chorus, the witness, the popularizer of the drama, it loses itself . . . ; as subject, it is thrown outside of itself, beyond itself [. . .] For it is possible that the last one without chorus, as I want to imagine him, would die, dead to himself, at the infinite twilight he would be. . . ." I have commented on these lines

knowing how we are able to think of our language—and to practice it—as the language of the survivor, or better as a surviving language: a language that is already situated beyond its own loss and nevertheless is able to experience and to inscribe that loss within itself. Or in other words again: we should be able to make our language speak from beyond its own death and at the same time, by the same token, to understand it as a space where the still born child shows up, manifests itself.

But there is a third series of questions, which, in turn, is related to literature and the structure of repetition that functions within literature, from novel to novel, from one author to another, or in the same novel, literally. What is ultimately the privilege of the novel, of what we call the novel? What we have said up to now does not give us the indispensable tools that would allow us to answer that question. With the figure of the still born child, we have stayed too close to the psychoanalytic vocabulary, at the risk of confusing everything. It is well known that the psychoanalytic approach has never been able to create a satisfying conceptuality for literature, and it would have a hard job creating it today for the structure of repetition in literature, for the experience of the Foreign, and for the inscription of a language's own death within itself. We therefore have to make a final leap, in order to dissipate the confusion, with the vague hope that the first two series of questions will also receive something close to an answer. This leap will bring us outside of the Armenian-speaking world, in search of a different horizon.

---

in the essay (in Armenian), *Anmardkayini P'ordzenkalumë* [*The Experience of Inhumanity*], published in my most recent book *Patker, Patum, Patmut'iun* (Yerevan: ActualArt, 2015). This essay was itself the expanded version of a lecture pronounced in English at UCLA in 2013, in the framework of a colloquium on "Inhumanities."

Before performing this exercise, one more word on the structure of repetition in *Asphalt* will be appropriate. We have already said that one way of reading this repetition was to suppose that the repeated sentences belonged to different contexts, one being the sphere of Nicole, the other one the sphere of Monique. The sentences, through this change of context, would also have incurred a change of signification. They would in both cases tell of the birth of the still born child, or its death. For a still born child, birth and death coincide. They would consequently foretell this coincidence between birth and death. But they would not tell it in the same context. The coincidence would not necessarily have the same meaning here and there. Now this change of meaning—assuming that there is such a change—is not in itself of a novelistic nature. It is not part of what the novel tells through its narrative, the protagonist is not concerned by this change. If we were in the framework of a classical novel, the protagonist would himself be transformed by this change, he would understand, at least implicitly, what has happened. Here, on the contrary, repetition works in and for itself, so to speak, independently of the protagonist.

II.

In order to better understand the nature of that repetition and transformation, we must now take into consideration what happens in one of Borges's stories, the one titled "Pierre Ménard, Author of the *Quixote*," which was first published in a literary journal in 1939, then in a collection of stories in 1941, and finally in the volume called *Ficciones* in 1944.[10]

[10]"Pierre Ménard" in Jorge Luis Borges, *Collected Fictions*, trans. Andrew Hurley, London: Penguin,

We know that Borges imagines a contemporary French writer, Pierre Ménard, who decided to re-experience the writing of Cervantes's *Quixote* word for word and in this way produces two chapters (the chapters nine and thirty-eight of the first part) and some other passages of Cervantes's work. Borges says that he was inspired by Novalis, and, more precisely, by one of Novalis's aphorisms, about the necessity of identifying oneself, of becoming one, with the author. In Borges's words,

> Two texts, of distinctly unequal value, inspired the undertaking. One was the philological fragment by Novalis—number 2005 in the Dresden edition, to be precise—which outlines the notion of total identification with a given author. The other was one of those parasitic books that set Christ on a boulevard, Hamlet on La Cannebière, or don Quixote on Wall Street.[11]

Before turning to this fragment by Novalis, we need to first understand that Pierre Ménard's idea is not to copy out the *Don Quixote*. Not to copy it out, but to repeat it word for word, which means: to re-experience and to reinvent from the inside the necessity of every word used and written down by Cervantes. In order to reach this point, he needs to push the identification to its most extreme possibility, to consider all the variants that could have occurred in Cervantes's mind and to follow the path that brought the author to his final choice of words in the *Don Quixote*. Borges is very clear. It's not a question of becoming Cervantes, of transforming oneself into someone else. Pierre Ménard has to remain who he is, a contemporary author, and he must arrive to the Quixote "through his own

1998, p. 88-95. An Armenian translation has been prepared for me by Vartan Matiossian, and published on the website of the journal *Ink'nagir* in 2015.

[11]*Collected Fictions*, p. 90. Subsequent references will be given in the body of the essay.

experiences." When he writes the Quixote in the 20th century, and not at the beginning of the 17 century, he transforms it into something absolute; he reinvents it not contingently as Cervantes had done, but necessarily. He reinvents the contingent text, plus its internal necessity. Cervantes's writing was simply anecdotal, haphazardly written down, or so it seems as long as that internal necessity had not been rediscovered. Moreover in the 17th century, the *Quixote* was written in a language that was entirely accessible to its readers. In the 20th century, the same *Quixote*, re-written in Spanish, (in Cervantes's Spanish), by a French author, becomes an improbable object. It recreates the genre of the historical novel, without any local color and any exoticism. It's the same work, physically, the same words, the same letters, and nevertheless it's a different work, given that the context of its production is not the same. Even the style is different. Cervantes's style was natural. Pierre Ménard's style, when he rewrites the *Quixote* in Spanish, is antiquated.

Thus, here is a magnificent musing on behalf of Borges, under the pretext of a critical article concerning Pierre Ménard's work; a musing of which the inspiration of course comes to him directly from the reflections of the first generation of German Romantics, the one regrouped in Iena around Friedrich Schlegel, with Novalis, Schelling, their wives and mistresses. The repetition that we have read in Vorpouni's novel does not spring from the same source of inspiration and does not obey the same principles; this is obvious. In both cases, it is true, the same text is transferred from one context to the other. In both cases, the language remains the same. But in Vorpouni's novel, the transfer is carried out in the same work and, it seems, by the same author. The central operation in the novel is precisely this strange transfer, through which the Still Born child appears and disappears. But conversely in both cases, an author translates that which another author (or the same) had written, in the same language. Consequently what commands this parallel, this juxtaposition, between Pierre Ménard and Vorpouni, is the need to understand this act— translating while remaining in the same language.

Should this transfer be read as a translation? At first glance, the connection between Borges's musing and the questions raised by translation—the very act of translating— is not obvious. But now here is Novalis's fragment, the one to which Borges makes an explicit reference, titled "Doctrine about the duties of a reader":

> Nur dann zeig' ich, dass ich einen Schriftsteller verstanden habe, wenn ich in seinem Geiste handeln kann; wenn ich ihn, ohne seine Individualität zu schmälern, übersetzen und mannigfach verändern kann.

> I show that I have correctly understood an author if and only if I am in the position of acting according to his spirit, when I can translate him without reducing his individuality, and when I can transform him in multiple directions.[12]

Novalis's preoccupation here is with the reader, the duties incumbent upon a reader, who should be able to entirely recreate a text for himself, to multiply it, to raise it to the second or the third power. Every reading in this sense is already philology, according to Novalis. And because the author is his/

[12]Novalis, *Fragmente*, Dresden: Wolfgang Jess, 1929, p. 644.

her first reader, every text contains in itself its own secret philology. In this short reflection under Novalis's pen, we already have one of the tenets of the Iena school, a tenet that is sometimes expressed in the form of an imperative or an injunction by Friedrich Schlegel or Novalis himself: the literary text must contain within itself its own explicitation, its own philological interpretation. Novalis's ideal was the text raised to an infinite power, in which what is literary and what is philological should mix and merge, to the point of being indistinguishable. This is how we, as writers, readers, or interpreters, belong more than ever to the horizon opened up by the Romantics. In that sense, Borges was their first and greatest heir. But in the fragment that we just read Novalis also speaks of the philological act of reading as though it were a translation. "I show that I have correctly understood an author if and only if . . . I can translate him."

At first glance, it seems Novalis uses the word "translate" here metaphorically, since he is preoccupied with the comprehension of a given text. Reading as a philological act contains within itself or presupposes an act of translation, which remains within the same language. The metaphor seems to generalize the usual sense of the word "translation." And we know that this is what Novalis had in mind, in his encyclopedic writings, a sort of general and reciprocal transfer between meanings, forms, and discourses. In that perspective, translation was the philological activity par excellence, because it was one of the privileged ways of infiniticizing the work of art.[13] But what the fragment

[13]On this idea of a general transferability and translatability "of everything into everything," which characterizes Novalis's "encyclopedic" writings and Friedrich Schlegel's project of a "progressive universal poetry," see Antoine Berman, *The Experience of the Foreign, Culture and Translation in Roman-*

says can also be understood without any mention of the ways of making the work of art infinite. Novalis demands from the reader (as translator) that he reproduce the work itself, not only the words and the sentences that comprise it, but also, and before all, the intention that gave birth to them, and consequently their internal necessity, the way it has been experienced and implemented by the author. It is precisely this demand for recreating the intention and the literal necessity that is recorded by Borges, when the latter makes Pierre Ménard write the following as an explanation for his crazy enterprise: "This game of solitaire I play is governed by two polar rules: the first allows me to try out formal or psychological variants; the second forces me to sacrifice them to the 'original' text and to come, by irrefutable arguments, to those eradications . . ." (93).

We can also consider what Maurice Blanchot, the greatest of all readers, wrote on Pierre Ménard's enterprise in the essay that he devoted to Borges and his "literary infinite" in his book of essays published in 1959, *Le Livre à venir*:

> When Borges suggests that we imagine a contemporary French author writing, starting with thoughts that are his own, somes pages that would textually reproduce two chapters of Don Quixote, this memorable absurdity is nothing other than that which is carried out in every translation. In a translation, we have the same work in two different languages: in Borges's fiction, we have two works in the identity of the same language, and in this identity, which is not one, the fascinating mirage of the duplicity of possible worlds.[14]

tic Germany, trans. Stefan Heyvaert, Albany: SUNY Press, 1992 (*L'Epreuve de l'étranger*, Gallimard, Tel, 1984) esp. Chapter 5, "Romantic Revolution and Infinite Versability."

[14]Maurice Blanchot, *Le Livre à venir*, Gallimard, 1959, pp. 118-119. *The Book to Come*, trans. Charlotte Mandell, Stanford University Press, p. 95.

To be sure, Blanchot's intention here was not exactly the same as ours in the present context. What interested him was the disparition of the original and the redoubling of the world "in a book." And, indeed, immediately after the lines that we just quoted, he says the following: "Thus, the world, if it could be exactly translated and copied in a book, would lose all beginning and all end and would become that spherical, finite, and limitless volume that all men write and in which they are written: it would no longer be the world; it would be the perverted world in the infinite sum of its possibles." What Blanchot describes or imagines here is the world of the eternal return, with just a slight correction. He describes the eternal return in which repetition occurs through translation. The same comes back, again and again, infinitely, but translated, into another language or in the same language. But what we call "translation," the demand for translation, is a demand that comes from the literary work as such. It is an imperative, which is hidden in the deepest folds of literature, and of which the echo has passed from the Romantics to Nietzsche, from Nietzsche to Borges, from Borges to Blanchot, and from Blanchot to us. A literary work is literary just as far as it has performed within itself the experience of translation, before every intervention of a real translator, in other words: as far as it has already met the Foreign within itself, from the start.

In his book *The Experience of the Foreign*, Antoine Berman had a formulation very close to this one, in his description and analysis of the theory of translation among the German Romantics. For them, the translating operation frees the work of art from the naturality of its language, it produces it a second time, it brings it to a second power, and by so doing it makes it more artificial, it raises it to the absolute of art. Berman—while criticizing the will of absolute, which according to him ignores the concreteness of languages—writes the following about this conception and this practice of translation: "Doesn't such a potentiating translation presuppose a relation of the work to its language and to itself that is itself of the order of translation, thus calling for, making possible, and justifying the movement of its translation?" And further on, "The work is that linguistic production which *calls* for translation as a destiny of its own. Let us provisionally name this call translatability."[15]The idea of this particular repetition inspired by the Romantics, of this call, which constitutes the core of a literary work, came to Antoine Berman straight from Walter Benjamin, and more precisely from his famous essay on the task of the translator. If a text is literary, it is due to the fact that it is *überstzbar*, let us say "translatable." This is what we read already under Benjamin's pen. But "translatable" does not have exactly the meaning that we usually give. It does not mean that it can be translated. It means that it contains within itself the demand of being translated. It's an injunction, a call. It screams: Translate me!

In Benjamin's essay, this is posed in the form of a question, which is tantamount to a statement: "Is it not the case that the work bears its own translation, and if this is so . . . does it not demand of being translated?"[16] And here is Derrida's commentary on this statement: "The original requires translation even if no translator is there, fit to respond to this injunction, which is at the same time demand and desire in the very struc-

[15]These excerpts are on pages 177-178 and 201 in French, 111 and 135 of the English translation.
[16]Walter Benjamin, *Gesammelte Schriften*, Band IV-1, Francfot: Suhrkamp Verlag, IV-1, p. 10.

ture of the original."[17] Accordingly, Benjamin is speaking of a radical translatability, a contract between languages at the origin of languages, when he says that it is the "translatability" of the original that decides the coincidence of a translation with the "essence of its form." And at the end he claims, "When the text immediately belongs to the pure language, without intermediary signification . . . it is then that it is absolutely translatable." This absolute translatability is the one of the Scripture. But the literary text also participates in this phenomenon and has in itself a degree of translatability. "In a variable measure, all great texts—but in the greatest measure the Scripture—contain between the lines their possible translation."[18]

It is this radical translatability that Derrida precisely translates with the French word *traductibilité*, which we then need to distinguish from *traduisibilité*, which the translator of Derrida's text into English renders with *transferability*. The to-be-translated of the sacred text, its pure transferability, that is what would give *at the limit* the ideal measure for all translation. The sacred text assigns the task to the translator, and it is sacred inasmuch as it announces itself as transferable, simply transferable, *to be translated*, which does not always mean immediately translatable, in the common sense that was dismissed from the start. Perhaps it is necessary here to distinguish between the transferable and the translatable. ". . . Never are the call for translation, the debt, the task, the assignation, more imperious. Never is there anything more transferable, yet by reason of this indistinction of meaning and literality (*Wörtlichkeit*),

[17]See Jacques Derrida, *Psyché*, Galilée, 1987, p. 216, and in English: *Acts of religion*, edited by Gil Anidjar, New York: Routledge, 2010, p. 116.
[18]*Gesammelte Schriften*, Band IV-1, p. 20-21.

the pure transferable can announce itself, give itself, present itself, let itself be translated *as untranslatable.*"[19] Derrida merely paraphrases Benjamin, on the strong accent on the "sacred" of the sacred text. It is true that through its pure translatability, it is the sacred that gives its measure to the literary. But again conversely, and when we observe the phenomenon from the side of what we now call transferability, the sacred is nothing else but the extreme measure of the literary.

To-be-translated, this is the requirement of the literary work, as literary. The *to-be-translated* is waiting in it, from the beginning. Consequently it is there that the encounter with the Foreign is located. The Armenian writers in Paris have written down the modalities of this encounter through their personal experience, no doubt. But, when we look at it from the horizon of the *to-be-translated*, this encounter obviously is located far beyond the personal experience. It is an encounter and an experience without a subject. It is there that a language reaches its limit, inscribes within itself its limit with all other languages, and consequently with itself as well— in other words, experiences and experiments its singularity and its difference.

What is then the encounter with the Foreign? Where does the privilege of the literary come from, when it is a question of defining this encounter? These were the questions that we asked ourselves previously. Here, with the experience of its singularity and its difference, a given language also experiences its other, its possible loss. This is why there is a potential loss in all languages, secretly waiting in them. Which certainly does

[19]*Psyché*, p. 234, *Acts of Religion*, p. 132.

not mean that all languages are lost in the Foreign. The loss of a language can be the object of an examination with the methods of sociology and sociolinguistics. A given language can be placed on the list of endangered languages, these languages that supposedly are under the threat of extinction. It is even possible to worry about its possible disappearance and take measures in order to prevent such a deadly outcome. These are justified and respectable approaches. But they say nothing, absolutely nothing about the negative potentiality, the potential loss, and they say nothing either about the experience of such a loss. Only the literary and sacred translatability, in the sense defined by Benjamin and Derrida, can provide the possibility and the reality of that experience. Only through the translatibility of the text—literary and sacred—does a given language experience itself as *surviving*. And this experience is located in the work and the text, before any intervention of a subject, and of course before any intervention of a real translator or translation. This is the way a given language experiments within itself its own loss, possible or effective.

It would be beneficial to pause here and provide a summary of what he have explored up until now. At the beginning we described a structure of repetition in the works of Vorpouni and Borges, and we asked some questions about the encounter with the foreign and the hypothetical privilege of literature. We then developed the problematic of translatability and transferability, on the footsteps of Benjamin and those who were directly inspired by him. There is something strange in this state of affairs. I will try to explain this as clearly as I can. The strangeness of the situation is the following: what we call translatability is a desire, a requirement, a call, an injunction, which originates in the work itself, but which remains in the dimension of pure potentiality—the passage from potentiality to actuality. The fact that a literary text is translated or not is entirely dependent on external conditions, and consequently has nothing to do either with the experience of the foreign, or with the self-experience of a given language as surviving. I am not claiming that the effectivity of translation is entirely left to chance, to fortuitous circumstances. What I am saying is that the decision to translate a work written in a given language can only come from someone who lives in a different language, who is the inhabitant of a language that is foreign to the language of the original, and this is true even if this *translator-to-be* is perfectly bilingual and even if he is motivated by the very subjective desire to make a work better known to a large public. Translatability is inherent in the language of the original. Should we therefore consider it as a paradox if I say that the translations of a work into foreign languages have nothing to do with the translatability hidden and awaiting in the work itself, the *to-be-translated* that constitutes the core of a literary work as literary?

If I decided to translate into French one of Vorpouni's novels, I would have to take into consideration the conditions of its reception in the French language. I wouldn't make any demands on the secret translatability within the literary work. And if we want to push this paradox to its farthest limit, we would even say that every translation, in that sense, betrays the translatability of the work. This very simple but admittedly highly paradoxical state of affairs begs a number of questions:

How is the encounter with the foreign brought about by the act of translation itself (and not simply by the secret translatability of the work)? How does one make a language experience its singularity and its difference with all other languages and with itself; how to make it repeat the experience of the work—an experience without a subject—through its translation? How to make translation and translatability coincide? What to do in order for translatability not to stay a pure potentiality? It is clear that the foreign translator must through her own work participate in the deepest layer of the work's experience in the translated language. Again how is this possible? How can a foreign translator inhabit both her own (foreign) language and the language of the original, provided that the language of the original for her is a foreign language, even if this translator is perfectly bilingual? It seems that we are faced with a requirement that is impossible to satisfy. Borges wanted precisely to meet this impossibility head on, he wanted to make this impossibility possible, or to inscribe this open abyss, this unbridgeable chasm between translation and translatability, in the archives of humanity.

I said earlier, at least twice now, "Even if the translator is perfectly bilingual." With the figure of Pierre Ménard, Borges presupposes the existence of a translator who is absolutely bilingual. He imagines the existence of a French translator who masters the Castilian language better that any Spanish contemporary, given that he is able to write that language just the way they spoke and wrote it at the beginning of the 17th century. Castilian is not his mother tongue; he learned it. He didn't learn it in the womb of his mother. It is even possible to say that his mastery of Castilian is better than Cervantes's mastery of his own mother tongue, which, after all, was only a natural language. He thus lays bare the non-naturality of the literary. Let me add, such a mastery is not entirely impossible. After all, the Mekhitarist Fathers of the 19th century, settled in their monasteries in Venice and Vienna, claimed that they wrote *grabar*, or classical Armenian, better than the authors of the 5th century. Their intention was to re-create the natural language, both written and spoken, of fifteen centuries ago, just the way it was written and spoken at that time, in its supposed purity, as though so many centuries had not passed since. And when Arsen Pakradouni was writing *Hayg the Hero* exactly the way it would have been written in the 5th century (but actually was not written), we are not that far from the delirious enterprise imagined by Borges. And why did Borges feel the need to imagine a French writer and place him at the center of his narrative, and not say a Spanish writer? The answer is easy now. The foreign translator had to participate with his work in the most intimate experience of the original language, in the encounter with the foreign as it could have been experienced and was never experienced as such in the original language, in the possibilities and the accidents provided by the translatability of the original. A foreign author, as foreign, had to make actual that which otherwise would have remained pure potentiality. Translation, in the form of a pure repetition, this way became the actual experience of translatability.

We must confess that Borges's dream is impressive. But then what happens in Vorpouni's novel is still more impressive, even if less visible to the naked eye. And, as a consequence, we need to meditate one more moment on what happens in Borges's narrative. Cervantes writes in the Spanish language of his epoch. He writes a natural and living language. As to Pierre Ménard, he writes in a language that is purely artificial. He writes the same work, the same chapters, the same words, but he doesn't write them in a living language. What he writes is the Castilian of three hundred years ago. It's not even a foreign language. It is explicitly a surviving language. Pierre Ménard writes that language as though it were still a living language. Or, on the contrary, he writes a living language as though it were dead. What matters then is not the fact that we have two different authors. What matters is that the language in which Don Quixote is written, here and there, does not have the same status. The language is the same, it is the same Castilian, and nevertheless its nature has changed radically when it passed from Cervantes to Pierre Ménard. It's not Cervantes national and natural language any more.

Now if we want to understand the structure of repetition in Vorpouni's work with the same categories, do we need to imagine that the one who writes and the one who repeats are two different authors, two different Vorpounis? The first one would be the Armenian one, the second one would be, let us say French. The French one would have usurped Vorpouni's name. He would have learned Armenian as a foreign language and would have made it his own language to such an extent that now the Armenian Vorpouni and the French Vorpouni would be indistinguishable, just like Cervantes and Pierre Ménard, not as subjects, but as authors. This other Vorpouni could have even written books in French. Why not? Others have done so instead of him. Shahnour has published poetry in French under the name of Armen Lubin, and no one at Gallimard knew at that time that he was a famous Armenian novelist. The second Vorpouni would have wanted to push the identification even farther, since he was now signing his books with the same name as the first Vorpouni. He copied the works of the first one, he wrote the same novel in a different context. Like Pierre Ménard, it was from his own experiences that he deduced the necessity of the text that had been written a first time by the first Vorpouni. And we could say about him what Borges says about Ménard, with just a small substitution, "Vorpouni's *Asphalt*" instead of "Cervantes's *Don Quixote*": "I shall turn now to the other, the subterranean, the interminably heroic production—the oeuvre non pareil, the oeuvre that remains—for such are our human limitations! —unfinished. This work, perhaps the most significant writing of our time, consists of the first and second chapter of Vorpouni's *Asphalt* and a fragment of chapter 3. I know that such a claim is on the face of it absurd . . ."[20]

Did I say "in a different context" a moment ago? Yes, it is clear that a work written in Armenian cannot be the same if the author is named Vorpouni and if he is named, let us say, Pierre Ménard alias Vorpouni. And just as Ménard did not want to be Cervantes and preferred to come to the Quixote "through the experiences of Pierre Ménard," we must imagine that the other Vorpouni, the usurper, preferred to remain who he was and come to *Asphalt* through his experiences of a French writer of the 20th century. If my auditors see a slight contradiction here,

[20]*Collected Fictions*, p. 90.

let me say that the same contradiction is to be found in Borges, where Ménard strives to a total identification as the writer of the Don Quixote, but not as a person. The same strange situation could be reproduced with the two Vorpounis. The first one would write his natural and national language. The second one would write in the same language, but as *a surviving language*. And immediately we see that what matters, once again, is the change of status of the language used. In the case imagined by Borges, a distance of three centuries was necessary between Cervantes and Ménard, in order for the latter's language to appear as a surviving language; whereas in Vorpouni's work the change is brought about on the spot and is recorded in the narrative. This change of status imposes itself as the real subject and the real object of the story.

Was this hypothesis of two Vorpounis intervening in the structure of repetition absurd? Maybe. But it is not more absurd than the one imagined by Borges. I can even say that it is a pretty faithful description of what happens, and, by the same token, a means of understanding retrospectively what was happening in Borges's narrative. Through the structure of repetition, what we have called absolute translatability (which was otherwise condemned to remain pure potentiality) becomes actual and represents the encounter with the foreign, now recorded in black and white. What else could we await from a novel whose aim was to be written in the surviving language, in the language of the survivor, I mean: to be written in such a way that the language in which it is written becomes a surviving language through the very fact that it is written and resonates from beyond its death. When Borges invents his Ménard, he invents a figure through which the impossible coincidence between translation and translatability would become reality, the potentiality would become actual, the secret encounter with the foreign would be brought about in and through the act of translating, by way of repetition pure and simple. This was Borges. With Vorpouni, it is not an invention any more. It is not imagined. The change of status of the language really happens. We have almost lost our tongue in the foreign. From now on we will write in the same language, but as a surviving language, the language of the absolute survivor.

When Hölderlin inscribed his famous sentence, the "almost" precisely signified the potentiality of the encounter with the foreign. His tongue had within itself the power of being lost. This is what I called a negative potentiality. Today, for us, for the absolute survivor, there is no "almost" any more. The loss has become quite real. The written language of the novel has become, through the very writing of the novel, a surviving tongue. It came to survive by way of its repetition in the novel. The loss in question is not a sociological fact any more. It manifests itself in a literary work and through the structure of repetition that is active within that work. In that sense, *Asphalt* is eminently the novel of the survivor, maybe more than *The Candidate* for example. From now on, we live in that country called loss. We live in it through our tongue, the language that we are writing and in which we are writing.

Where and when can a language be considered "lost"? The answer is: when it does not translate any more. Western Armenian has ceased to translate for eight or nine decades. Its last great translator was Arsen Ghazikian. After him, I know only one author who practiced translation on an ongoing basis, Yervant Gobelian, who is not well known outside of the community where he was active as an intellectual, the Armenian community of Istanbul. In any case, Western Armenian does not translate any more, so it is. The experience of loss consequently could be registered or recorded only in a literary production committed to a creative confrontation with translation, with the contextual and transcendental impossibility of translating into Western Armenian. This is how the encounter with the foreign leads to the paradoxical birth of the Still Born child, through the structure of repetition that lays bare the translating movement and its final failure. What happens here is also of course a lesson for all other languages, which have not yet reached that outcome, that failure, that measure in their experience of the foreign. For instance Pierre Ménard's French, Cervantes's Spanish, or Hölderlin's German, and why not also Armenian, when considered a national language, a language that has not yet gone through the experience of the still born, of a birth aborted for ever. Because the abortion of the translating movement secretly waits at the horizon of all languages. These languages should learn that if it is always possible to translate between national languages, even if that translating passage from the one to the other is always respectable, even if it is a historical necessity (which began to be felt on a large scale only with the advent of national languages, precisely in the time of Goethe's *Weltliteratur*), it is nevertheless true that the respectable act of translating between national languages does not have much to do with the act of translating into a surviving language—the one which translates into a living language as though it were dead, or into a dead language as though it were alive. Only that act of translation can lay bare the essence and the substance of a surviving language, as surviving.

We arrived at the limit. The end has begun. We must translate. It is an imperative. We must translate because the end has begun. But we now know that translation aborts if it does not take into consideration the change in status of our language. From now on, the imperative has also changed in nature. Henceforth it has become the imperative to translate into the language, our language, the same language, but as a surviving one. Who would have ever heard that imperative if we had not been confronted by the loss of our language in foreign countries?

Milena Abrahamyan is a feminist from the intersection of the west and the Other. She believes in the power womyn have. She is a poet because she is queer and queer because she is a poet. Milena considers Shushan Avagyan to be one of the most important contemporary feminist authors in Armenian time.

Ani Asatryan was born around the time of Armenia's independence from the Soviet Union. She studies art, literature, and is one of the most celebrated female writers in Armenia today. In 2014, her first "unreadable" book was published. This book attempted to break the conventional borders of literature and visual art in order to highlight the ties that exist between literary text, sound, image, and memory.

Shushan Avagyan (b. 1976) is the author of the novel *Girk-anvernagir* [*Book, Untitled*] (2006) and co-author of *Zarubyani Kanayq* [*The Women of Zarubyan*] (2014). She has translated several books into English, including *I Want to Live: Poems of Shushanik Kurghinian* (AIWA Press, 2005). Her articles and translations have appeared in *Context*, *Review of Contemporary Fiction*, *Music & Literature*, and *Dissidences: Hispanic Journal of Theory and Criticism*. She currently teaches at the American University of Armenia.

Christian Batikian is an Armenian author, born in Beirut and raised in Istanbul and Paris. He has been writing since his adolescent years, and has been published for over a decade in prominent journals, newspapers, and anthologies all over the world, not limited to: Paris, Istanbul, Armenia, and Lebanon. Batikian is a highly respected and loved author internationally, and composes his stories in Western Armenian, the dialect of Armenian that is currently on UNESCO list of endangered languages. He currently resides in Yerevan, Armenia.

Krikor Beledian is an Armenian poet, novelist, and literary critic born in Lebanon and living in France. His work has been published in Beirut, Paris, Yerevan, and Los Angeles. He teaches at the National Institute for Oriental Languages and Civilizations in Paris.

Tamar M. Boyadjian is Assistant Professor of Medieval Literature and Creative Writing in the English Department at Michigan State University. Her academic and creative research and teaching focuses on transcultural interactions between various ethno-religious cultures from the medieval to the contemporary period. She also teaches courses on translation and translation theory, with an emphasis on trauma, postcolonial studies, and endangered languages. Her poetry and scholarly work have been published widely all over the world.

Talar Chahinian holds a Ph.D. in Comparative Literature from UCLA and lectures in the Department of Comparative World Literature and Classics at California State University, Long Beach. She is the co-editor of *Diaspora: A Journal of Transnational Studies*.

Anna Davtyan is a writer, translator and photographer born in Armenia. She is the author of the bilingual (Armenian, English) poetry collection *Book of Gratitude* (Yerevan, 2012). Her translation projects feature the works of the Beat Generation--Allen Ginsberg, William S. Burroughs, Jack Kerouac, and others. Davtyan's drama A *Shipload of Carnations for Hrant Dink* was staged by the German theater Krefeld und Monchengladbach in September 2016.

Dzovinar Derderian is a PhD Candidate at the University of Michigan in Ann Arbor focusing on nineteenth-century Ottoman history.

Alec Ekmekji wanted to become a writer when he was a teenager. Instead he studied physics and mathematics in college and worked as an engineer in the defense industry, working to keep the free world free. After the fall of the Soviet Union he turned to writing poetry and short stories again, and to translating Armenian poetry into English.

Violet Grigoryan was born in Tehran before her family repatriated in Armenia in 1975. She was one of the founders of the literary journal *Inknagir*, for which she currently serves as its editor. The author of four books of poems, Grigoryan has won the Writers' Union of Armenia poetry award for [*True, I'm*

Telling the Truth] (1991), and the Golden Cane prize in literature for [*The City*] (1998). Her poems have been anthologized in France, and in the English-language collections *The Other Voice: Armenian Women's Poetry Through the Ages* (2006) and *Deviation: Anthology of Contemporary Armenian Literature* (2008).

Nairi Hakhverdi is a translator, writer, and editor. She grew up in the Netherlands where she attended international schools and earned a degree in English language and literature. In 2009, she moved to Armenia, where she taught literary translation at Yerevan State Linguistic University for three years. She has translated numerous classical and contemporary Armenian authors into English, and her works have appeared in several international publications, including *Words Without Borders*, *Asymptote*, and *City Books*. In 2017, her translations of two novels, Aram Pachyan's *Goodbye Bird* and Hovhannes Tekgyozyan's *Fleeting City*, were respectively published by Glagoslav Publications and Mosaic Press.

Vahan Ishakhanian—the compiler of the Armenian text—is a writer who resides in Armenia and is the author of many journalistic articles, blogs, and books.

Karen Jallatyan is a Comparative Literature Ph.D. candidate from University of California, Irvine. His research interests are cinema and contemporary Armenian literatures in relation to other literary and artistic traditions.

Narine Jallatyan is a Ph.D. student in the department of Comparative Literature at UCLA. Her fields of interest include 20th-century Anglophone and Francophone Caribbean poetry and the poetic production of the Armenian Diaspora within the theoretical framework of post-colonial and diaspora studies. Her research explores ways in which the discourse of poetry thinks, feels, or overcomes the impact of a traumatic past on language that bears the marks of such a past. Narine has an M.A degree in Comparative Literature and a B.A degree in International Development Studies, both from UCLA.

Shushan Karapetian is a lecturer in the department of Near Eastern Languages and Cultures at UCLA. Her dissertation, *"How Do I Teach My Kids My Broken Armenian?": A Study of Eastern Armenian Heritage Language Speakers in Los Angeles*, won the Society for Armenian Studies Distinguished Dissertation Award for 2011-2014. Her research interests focus on heritage languages and speakers, particularly on the case of Armenian heritage speakers in the Los Angeles community, about which she has presented and lectured widely.

Karén Karslyan is a poet, novelist, translator, musician, and a visual artist. He is the author of *Aterazma*, a typographic film (Inknagir, 2016), *Doomed to Spell*, a collection of 38 deformed *hayrens* (Inknagir, 2010), *X Frames/Sec*, a collection of works including a minimalist novel of the same name and poems (Bnagir, 2003). Armenia's public TV station declared him the Scandalous Writer of the Year 2003 for *X Frames/Sec*. He is the recipient of Young Artists Award for the manuscript of *Password*, a novel in progress. He is also the editor of the Armenian translation of *Hedgehog in the Fog*, a collection of fairy tales by Sergey Kozlov (2016). He received his PhD in English from the National Academy of Sciences of the Republic of Armenia. (More at www.karenkarslyan.com).

Lilit Keshishyan holds a Ph.D. in Comparative Literature from the University of California, Los Angeles. Her academic work explores the intricacies and challenges posed by issues of identity, language, and place in the literature of the Armenian diaspora.

Raymond Boghos Kupelian (1936-), born in Iskenderun, has been writing fiction, short stories and essays since the mid-60's. His work brings the experience and keen appreciation of the various worlds he has encountered from Africa to the Middle East. His novels, short stories and essays have been translated into a number of different languages including English, Russian and Arabic. Having lived both in Lebanon and Sierra Leone, Kupelian now makes his home in Los Angeles.

Roger Kupelian is an independent filmmaker who, partly inspired by his childhood in Sierra Leone, creates worlds using words, images and visual effects. A 23-year veteran of the Hollywood Visual Effects machine, he has worked on many Hollywood blockbuster films, such as Peter Jackson's *Lord of the Rings* trilogy. He is a proud bookworm, and creator of his own *East of Byzantium* graphic novel series.

Marc Nichanian is a philosopher and literary scholar who has taught in France (University of Strasbourg), the United States (UCLA and Columbia University), Turkey (Sabanci University), and now Armenia (AUA). He is the author of a history of the Armenian language and a multivolume history of 20th century Armenian literature. His most recent publications include in Turkish: *Edebiyat ve Felaket* [Literature and Catastrophe] (Iletişim, 2011), in English: *The Historiographic*

Perversion (Columbia University Press, 2009), *Mourning Philology* (Fordham University Press, 2014), in French: *Le Sujet de l'histoire* (Lignes, 2015), in Armenian: *Patker, patum, patmut'iun* [Image, narrative, history] in two volumes (ActualArt, Yerevan, 2015-16), and most recently *Nietzsche, vasn inqnishkhanoutean* [Nietzsche, the will to sovereignty] (Inknagir, 2017). He has translated works from Maurice Blanchot, Friedrich Nietzsche, Georges Bataille, Walter Benjamin, into (Western) Armenian.

Aram Pachyan was born on March 19, 1983, to a family of doctors. He studied law at Yerevan State University in Armenia between 1999 and 2004. After graduating, he began to write short stories and essays, which were eventually published in Armenian magazines, including *Literary Journal*, *Gretert*, and *Yeghitsi Luys*. He is the author of two collections of short stories, "*Robinson*" and *Ocean*, and of the novel, *Goodbye, Bird*. His works have been translated into English, Ukrainian, and Russian.

Michael Pifer is a National Endowment for the Humanities Fellow at the University of Michigan; he is currently writing a literary history of medieval Anatolia. His recent publications include *An Armenian Mediterranean: Words and Worlds in Motion* (Palgrave Macmillan, 2018), which he co-edited with Kathryn Babayan.

Ikna Sarıaslan is a highly celebrated Armenian poet whose work reflects on questions of love, identity, and the city of Istanbul. He currently resides in Turkey, where he serves on the PEN Turkey board.

Vehanoush Tekian was born in Beirut in 1948 and has studied Philosophy and English Literature in the American University of Beirut. She has started writing early on, contributing to various diaspora Armenian periodicals. Currently residing in New Jersey, Tekian has published 11 volumes of prose and poetry.

Maroush Yeramian is a contemporary Armenian author and teacher; in her succinct style, she describes herself as a poet of Aleppo.

Ara Kazandjian (1967) was born in Anjar, Lebanon. He received his primary and secondary education in Anjar before enrolling in summer courses (in Venice, Italy) organized by the Mekhitarist Congregation and then by the Venice State University. In 1990, Kazandjian moved to Los Angeles, where he received his BA in Armenian Studies from the Armenian American International College at the University of La Verne. Afterward, he joined the editorial staff of the bilingual newspaper, *Asbarez*. He has taught courses in Armenian Language and History since 1994. Among his publications are *Ket* (1993), *In the Showcase* (1997), and *Doghargakh* (2015), as well as a myriad of poems and articles that have been appeared in diasporan and Armenian newspapers.

www.ingramcontent.com/pod-product-compliance
Lightning Source LLC
LaVergne TN
LVHW051515070426
835507LV00023B/3123
* 9 7 8 1 6 0 7 8 5 4 8 0 7 *